Historic Hotels & Hideaways

A WASHINGTON WEEKENDS BOOK,
A series of two-day adventures in and around Washington, D.C.—
Each based on a travel theme. Other titles include:

Breaking Away to Virginia and Maryland Wineries
by Elizabeth Frater

Historic Hotels & Hideaways

TRISH FOXWELL

CAPITAL
BOOKS, INC.
Sterling, Virginia

Capital Books, Inc.
P.O. Box 605
Herndon, Virginia 20172-0605

ISBN 1-931868-16-6 (alk. paper)

Photographs © by Trish Foxwell and Steve Foxwell unless otherwise noted.

Library of Congress Cataloging-in-Publication Data

Foxwell, Trish.
    Historic hotels & hideaways / Trish Foxwell.
       p. cm.
    ISBN 1-931868-16-6 (alk. paper)
      1. Hotels—Middle Atlantic States—Guidebooks. 2. Bed and breakfast
accommodations—Middle Atlantic States—Guidebooks. 3. Middle Atlantic
States—Guidebooks. I. Title: Historic hotels and hideaways. II. Title.

TX907.3.M53F69   2003
647.94—dc21

                          2003005177

Printed in the United States of America on acid-free paper that meets the American National Standards Institute Z39-48 Standard.

First Edition

10 9 8 7 6 5 4 3 2 1

This book is a tribute to my parents, whose love of adventure and travel played a significant role when I was envisioning *Historic Hotels & Hideaways*. My father, a naval officer, traveled the globe extensively, and luckily I got to go along for the thrilling ride. His love of storytelling inspired me early on to become a journalist and photographer, while my beautiful and talented mother would pack a suitcase at the drop of a hat to discover a new horizon. Her innate love of the finer things in life enabled me to experience some of the world's grandest hotels and hideaways, while never taking the journey for granted.

Together their desire to "see the world" became second nature to me as well and inspired me to write *Historic Hotels & Hideaways*. This is their story as well in so many ways, and each time I step inside many of these fine hotels and inns, fond memories of them will quickly surface and linger long afterward.

I also dedicate the book to my grandparents, Mr. and Mrs. John H. Myers, for putting many of my dreams within reach, and to my favorite author, F. Scott Fitzgerald, whose passionate love of travel and great hotels inspired many of his novels. My knowledge of his lengthy tenure at the Grove Park Inn in Asheville launched the book. No doubt many of his first and second drafts were penned on hotel stationery.

And finally, to the many illustrious individuals mentioned in the book who led such illuminating lives and without whom this book would not have been possible.

Contents

Preface   xi

Acknowledgments   xv

Introduction   xvii

CHAPTER 1   PENNSYLVANIA   1

Bucks County

     Barley Sheaf Farm   3
     Highland Farms Bed & Breakfast   5
     The Mansion Inn   7
     Excursions and Diversions   7

Gettysburg

     The Gettysburg Hotel   10
     Excursions and Diversions   12

Hershey

     The Hotel Hershey   13
     Excursions and Diversions   15

Philadelphia

     The Park Hyatt Philadelphia at the Bellevue   17
     The Best Western Independence Park Hotel   22
     The Latham Hotel   24
     Excursions and Diversions   25

York

     The Yorktowne Hotel   27
     Excursions and Diversions   28

CHAPTER 2   DELAWARE   31

Wilmington

>Hotel Du Pont   33
>The Inn at Montchanin Village   36
>*Excursions and Diversions*   37

CHAPTER 3   MARYLAND   41

Annapolis

>Historic Inns of Annapolis   43
>*Excursions and Diversions*   46

Baltimore

>Radisson Plaza Lord Baltimore Hotel   48
>Admiral Fell Inn   51
>Peabody Court Hotel   53
>*Excursions and Diversions*   54

Oxford

>The Robert Morris Inn   57
>*Excursions and Diversions*   59

Sharpsburg

>The Inn at Antietam   60
>*Excursions and Diversions*   61

St. Michaels

>The Inn at Perry Cabin   63
>*Excursions and Diversions*   65

Taneytown

>Antrim 1844 Inn   66
>*Excursions and Diversions*   67

CHAPTER 4   WASHINGTON, D.C.   69

>The Hay Adams   72
>The Henley Park Hotel   74

The Jefferson Hotel   76
The Mayflower Hotel   79
Morrison-Clark Inn   82
The Phoenix Park Hotel   84
The St. Regis   86
The Willard InterContinental Hotel   88
Excursions and Diversions   90

CHAPTER 5   VIRGINIA   93

Charlottesville
    The Boars Head Inn   95
    Keswick Hall   97
    Excursions and Diversions   98

Hot Springs
    The Homestead   101
    Excursions and Diversions   104

Hunt Country
    The Red Fox Inn (Middleburg)   107
    The Goodstone Inn (Middleburg)   111
    The Black Horse Inn (Warrenton)   113
    The Ashby Inn (Paris)   115
    Excursions and Diversions   116

Richmond
    The Jefferson Hotel   118
    Excursions and Diversions   123

Roanoke
    The Hotel Roanoke   125
    Excursions and Diversions   127

Virginia Beach
    The Cavalier Hotel   129
    Excursions and Diversions   132

Williamsburg

    The Williamsburg Inn   134

    Excursions and Diversions   135

CHAPTER 6   WEST VIRGINIA   139

White Sulphur Springs

    The Greenbrier   141

    Excursions and Diversions   148

CHAPTER 7   NORTH CAROLINA   151

Asheville

    The Grove Park Inn   153

    Excursions and Diversions   157

Chapel Hill

    The Carolina Inn   159

    Excursions and Diversions   161

Pinehurst

    Pinehurst   163

    Excursions and Diversions   166

Bibliography   169

Index   171

Preface

There is a certain magic attached to visiting and exploring historic inns and hotels. Discovering pieces of history and some of the fascinating individuals who shaped it is truly the most exciting and rewarding travel experience of all, particularly for historical travelers wanting to "scratch beneath the surface" on their adventures.

"If only these walls could talk." The time-worn phrase sums up why I began visiting and eventually writing about historic hotels and hideaways in the mid-Atlantic region. From Richmond's grand and glorious Jefferson Hotel to Middleburg's woodsy Red Fox Inn and Asheville's sprawling Grove Park Inn, history unfolds at every one of these properties.

Visiting the hotel where F. Scott Fitzgerald spent two summers, seeing where Jacqueline Kennedy traveled for a respite from her public life, and piecing together the many travels of Charles Lindbergh, the Vanderbilts, the Rockefellers, Gen. Robert E. Lee, golfing great Bobby Jones, architect Stanford White, Charlie Chaplin, and Eleanor and Franklin Roosevelt, along with a host of others, became the most interesting part of the journey. Countless other "icons of history" surfaced along the way, making the discovery all the more appealing and exciting.

To touch pieces of history became my primary objective in writing the book. A love of travel, architecture, history, and biography all came together when penning the first drafts. The search to explore these historic hotels began on an outing to Asheville where I wanted to discover where F. Scott Fitzgerald had lived for a brief period.

More stories began to unfold as I began the arduous task of piecing together the material. Not only did Fitzgerald live at the Grove Park Inn while his wife, Zelda, recuperated at nearby Highlands Hospital, but Thomas Edison, Henry Ford, and Franklin Roosevelt also made appearances at the venerable lodging establishment. Margaret Mitchell of *Gone with the Wind* fame was another name listed on the hotel's faded roster. Mitchell traveled to the woodsy enclave while on a honeymoon with her first husband. And the list goes on.

In short, American history and the many names associated with it came to the forefront on the fascinating journey encompassing every time period from the Civil War, the Gilded Age, the Roaring Twenties, the Great Depression, and into World War II and the sixties. All of these eras were discovered in this collection of magical places and revealed at every turn.

As a prerequisite, the hotels and inns selected for *Historic Hotels and Hideaways* had to have a historical background—a pedigree, if you will. Although there are numerous inns and hotels throughout the Mid-Atlantic that offer wonderful accommodations, they simply did not measure up when it came time to delve into their histories.

I concentrated on inns and hotels in places where travelers would want to go on a long weekend getaway, be it a historic hamlet, a country village, or a cosmopolitan city. The location and backdrop of the inn or hotel became as significant as the history of the property itself. These were places that I had discovered for myself to be special, and I wanted to share the information with readers who had an interest in history and historical figures. Civil War sites, hunt country, university towns, resorts, and cities were all added to the list, contributing to the variety of hotels and inns that make *Historic Hotels & Hideaways* different from other guidebooks.

While the obvious choices were the easy ones to highlight, the lesser-known hotels and inns came to the forefront as the book began taking shape. "Nuggets of history" began appearing everywhere from Philadelphia to Pinehurst.

And there were many surprises along the way as well. Bucks County, Pennsylvania became an artists' haven during the 1930s and '40s when many of Broadway's brightest composers camped out in the idyllic hideaway to score a number of theatrical hits far removed from the pressures of Manhattan. Did you know that George Kaufman, Oscar Hammerstein, and Moss Hart regularly met on weekends in the Pennsylvania countryside to score some of Broadway's most beloved theatrical productions? *Oklahoma, South Pacific, The King and I, The Man Who Came to Dinner,* and *Dinner at Eight* all took flight in Bucks County. That the legendary tap dancer "Bojangles" was first discovered while working as a waiter at Richmond's swanky Jefferson Hotel, and that the Duke and Duchess of Windsor had a particular fondness for the Cameo Ballroom at the Greenbrier? And that the Cornelius Vanderbilts and President and Mrs. Woodrow Wilson all traveled to the Homestead in Hot Springs, Virginia on their honeymoons?

These stories and many more are revealed within the pages of *Historic*

Hotels & Hideaways. While much has been written about the importance of restoring architectural landmarks, and many of these hotels and inns fall into that category, I wanted to tell a more personal story. To connect legendary individuals with these hotels and inns became a top priority. From presidents to inventors, royalty, composers, and movie stars—an illustrious cast of characters traveled to these diverse destinations and hideaways that artfully mirror the American landscape and experience.

So when you visit the Greenbrier and wander along its stately corridors, whispers of Gen. Robert E. Lee, the Duke of Windsor, and Grace Kelly may very well surface. Or when you step inside the Jefferson Hotel in Richmond, thoughts of silent screen star Charlie Chaplin, architect Stanford White, or aviator Charles Lindbergh might greet you. And if you happen to travel to Asheville, North Carolina, memories of F. Scott Fitzgerald will most certainly haunt you as you sit and gaze at the mountain landscape that became such a welcome refuge for the writer during his difficult summers there. These stories and many more can be found at these legendary old hotels and inns, which provide unmatched glimpses into pieces of the American story. A visit ensures a deeper and closer look at valuable fragments of the captivating American story and some of the famous names associated with these hotels and inns.

In short, visiting these places is the closest you might ever get to learning more about this fabled cast of characters who traveled to these extraordinary hotels and inns. Enjoy your discovery!

Acknowledgments

Historic Hotels and Hideaways would not have been possible without the assistance and expertise provided by the National Trust's Historic Hotels Group and in particular Mary Billingsley, who provided me with key information at every step. The staff's invaluable assistance in clarifying information at every turn helped me in shaping the contents of the book.

Historians Robert Conte at the Greenbrier Hotel and John Hoover at the Homestead provided me with valuable information and archival photographs. Jennifer Crisp, at the Jefferson Hotel, clearly went the "extra mile" in locating the photo of Elvis Presley and key documents related to Lindbergh's visit. Convention bureaus and tourism centers proved invaluable when the time came to piece together the archival material.

Special recognition should also be given to Vickie Bendure, representing Loudoun County, and J. Harry Feldman at the Wilmington, Delaware Convention and Visitors Bureau, who assisted greatly every step of the way in ensuring historical accuracy. J. Harry Feldman in particular was always at the ready in keeping me informed on all things related to the Brandywine River Valley and Wilmington.

In addition, my thanks go to Margaret Skinner at the Carolina Inn, Dave Tomsky, formerly of the Grove Park Inn, and so many other individuals not listed here who offered their invaluable expertise and information in crafting the book. Rick Cunningham of the Yorktowne Hotel was also of immeasurable help when piecing the information together.

Special mention should also be reserved for my aunts, Dr. Christine Sweeney and Miss Margaret Sweeney, whose prior work with the National Trust for Historic Preservation proved invaluable when the selection of inns and hotels for the book began. An extra acknowledgment should be given to my sister, Martha Welch, who has been consistently supportive of my creative endeavors.

And last, but certainly not least, thanks to my husband, Steve Foxwell, who gave up numerous weekends and evenings to assist me with fact checking, organizing, and finally typing the final manuscript. Without his loyalty, encouragement, and enthusiasm the book would never have been completed. The project became a labor of love for both of us in the early stages as we began exploring all of these wonderful hotels and inns. Stepping inside these legendary places that attracted such icons of history—from presidents to Hollywood greats to noted writers and dignitaries—added to the excitement.

It is our fervent hope that after reading *Historic Hotels & Hideaways* travelers with an interest in history will want to go out and search out these extraordinary places for themselves and discover a very important part of the American landscape.

Finally, thanks to all of the archivists, editors, reporters, visitors' bureaus, and hotel and travel contacts not mentioned and to individuals I have worked with over the years as a travel writer and newspaper reporter who inspired me in their own way to write *Historic Hotels & Hideaways.*

In closing, special mention should also be given to my publisher, Kathleen Hughes of Capital Books, and Judy Karpinski and Judy Coughlin, my editors, who all believed in the merit of *Historic Hotels & Hideaways* from the beginning and were willing to take a chance on my first attempt at writing a travel book.

Introduction

The beginning of each section in the book highlights distinguishing characteristics of the state and then swiftly moves into the towns and cities where the historic hotels and hideaways are located. The text concentrates mainly on the various inns or hotels mentioned, elaborating on interesting stories and personalities associated with the properties. Pertinent sidebar information at the end of the section makes it easier to find detailed information on the hotel or inn, including the approximate mileage from Washington, D.C., and driving time. The sidebar also includes a price index with dollar signs indicating the following:

$$—economical
$$$—moderate
$$$$—pricey
$$$$$—expensive

The Excursions and Diversions section provides important information about the day trips and sites mentioned so you can search the Web, write, or phone for up-to-date information. I have also tried to give as many toll-free numbers as possible both for the hotels and inns and for attractions, making it easier to get the information you want prior to your trip. In effect, you can wander from one state to another and get a fairly accurate idea of how to reach the inn, hotel, or excursion's beginning point. So whether you want to explore Virginia first and then head over to Maryland's Eastern Shore or opt for the Brandywine experience in Delaware, you can quickly scan for information before your trip. The Diversions section suggests the more interesting things to see and do while in the area, with sidebars again providing pertinent information. Having all of the information readily accessible and at your fingertips makes getting to these areas easier. Mileage and estimated driving time are also mentioned so that you can plan ahead and get a basic idea of what to expect in terms of travel times, distances, and so forth. Whether you begin your journey in

Washington or decide to discover the Brandywine, *Historic Hotels & Hideaways* will try to guide you to the most appealing day trips and excursions.

For instance, when you start exploring the nation's capital there are a host of engaging sites to see in addition to the obvious Smithsonian museums. The Woodrow Wilson home near Embassy Row along with the Marjorie Merriweather Post estate, Hillwood, reveal another chapter in Washington's rich historical legacy. In addition, on a tour through Bucks County or Asheville recommended sites to visit are highlighted. While Biltmore House is a must on a visit to Asheville, Thomas Wolfe's Old Kentucky Home provides travelers with a taste of Asheville's fascinating literary legacy.

By taking along *Historic Hotels & Hideaways,* you will be able to follow in the footsteps of history and the many individuals who shaped it and hopefully experience travel with a whole new perspective and outlook. In effect, you will touch valuable and vintage pieces of the American landscape that have shaped this great nation.

CHAPTER 1 *Pennsylvania*

BUCKS COUNTY
Barley Sheaf Farm

The Keystone State offers an abundance of activities and sites for travelers. From Philadelphia with the Liberty Bell and Independence Hall to Hershey, renowned for its delectable chocolates, and Gettysburg, site of the most famous Civil War battlefield, many historical facets are in store on a visit through Pennsylvania.

A serene countryside setting frames the entrance to Barley Sheaf Farm in Bucks County. *Barley Sheaf Inn*

Some of Broadway's brightest names from its Golden Age can be discovered on a swing through Bucks County.

Resplendent with farmhouses, winding country lanes, and a string of colonial villages, this area of Pennsylvania is an artists' haven and hangout.

P.O. Box 10
Holicong, PA 18928-0010
Tel: (215) 794-5104
www.barleysheaf.com
$$$
160 miles/3½ hours

George S. Kaufman, Oscar Hammerstein, and Moss Hart are the names most often bandied about in these parts. Literary links are also listed in its history—Pearl Buck made her home in New Hope following her exploits in China, and the James Michener Art Museum is named after the Doylestown native.

Peppered with art galleries, antique shops, and charm around every bend, Bucks County is a natural for both Washingtonians and Philadelphians (one hour away) desiring a country experience.

In the heart of bucolic Bucks County, you will find the Barley Sheaf Farm, former home of George S. Kaufman and creative inspiration behind the plays *Dinner at Eight* and *The Man Who Came to Dinner,* among others.

Former owner Peter Seuss, originally from Switzerland, purchased the Inn in 1994. He has added tasteful European touches, revamping and renovating the beautiful inn to reflect his attention to detail.

The Barley Sheaf continues to cater to the New York literary set and discerning urbanites who desire a weekend country setting. The fifteen-room inn continues to remind visitors of Kaufman and his literary legacy and of his many famous friends who frequented the inn while Kaufman was living here. Three buildings make up the complex, which consists of the main house with its seven guest rooms; the barn, offering five rooms; and the ultraprivate cottage, offering three bedrooms.

Situated on thirty sprawling acres, the Barley Sheaf offers some of the loveliest accommodations in Bucks County. A full country breakfast and afternoon tea add to the overall experience in between exploring the host of art galleries and antique shops that are conveniently situated nearby.

The Kaufman story is of course the main draw and most intriguing tale associated with the inn. The inn was originally owned by Juliana Force, the first woman director of New York's Whitney Museum of Art. The fabled history of the house began when she took over its ownership and added a new kitchen, a mansard roof, and a swimming pool.

The story goes that Kaufman noticed the house during a Sunday drive and offered Force $45,000 in 1936. The playwright made it his weekend retreat from 1936 until 1950. Some of New York's most famous glitterati gathered at the wooded estate, including Dorothy Parker, Alexander Woollcott, Oscar Hammerstein, John Steinbeck, the Marx Brothers, and Kaufman's close friend and collaborator Moss Hart.

Kaufman sold the house in 1950, and it remained a private residence until 1979, when it was turned into a bed-and-breakfast. The inn offers beautifully appointed guest rooms with a country-style décor, plush comfortable beds, and fireplaces in some rooms. Guests can opt to stay in Room One in the main house, where Kaufman penned many of his best known works.

The Barley Sheaf Farm

ACCOMMODATIONS: Fifteen-room bed-and-breakfast

DIRECTIONS: Barley Sheaf Farm is north of Philadelphia in Bucks County, Pennsylvania, about a three-and-a-half-hour drive from the Washington area. Take I-95 north to Trenton exit Route 332. At the top of the ramp make a left onto Route 332 west. After approximately four miles, this road will merge into Route 413 north. Follow Route 413 north for approximately ten miles; look for Route 263 in the Buckingham area. At the light make a right onto Route 263 north and go through two traffic lights. After you pass the second traffic light, the inn is on the right.

Highland Farms Bed & Breakfast

The two-hundred-year-old stone and stucco farmhouse, in one of Bucks County's choicest corners, was the former residence of the brilliantly talented lyricist Oscar Hammerstein, who lived here from 1940 until his death in 1960.

The former home of music great Oscar Hammerstein now awaits visitors to Highland Farms Bed & Breakfast. *Highland Farms*

Anyone with an interest in and appreciation for music should not bypass this gem of a weekend retreat. Hammerstein fell in love with the area and completed some of his most important works while living here, including the lyrics to *Oklahoma*, *The Sound of Music*, *Carousel*, and *Flower Drum Song*, among others. In fact, the bottom of the pear-shaped swimming pool displays the lyrics to *The Sound of Music*.

70 East Road
Doylestown, PA 18901
Tel: (215) 340-1354
www.web-comm.com/
  highland
$$$
161 miles/3½ hours

Hammerstein moved into the house with his wife and five children in 1940 when his career was at its zenith. Its proximity to New York City proved ideal for the lyricist, who traveled to the city frequently. The composer left the house to his wife, who sold it in 1961.

The privately owned Federal-style farmhouse is a member of the National Trust Historic Registry and has been open as a bed-and-breakfast since 1984. The memories of Hammerstein are found everywhere in the twenty-one-room inn, which offers five guest rooms. The rooms that are open to the public pay homage to Hammerstein and are named appropriately after his most famous Broadway creations. The Carousel bedroom and The King & I bedroom, Showboat, and Oklahoma guest rooms feature themes related to the Broadway shows. Old photographs, vintage sheet music, and other memorabilia related to the acclaimed lyricist can be enjoyed on a visit. Hammerstein's famous friends frequented the house, including Moss Hart, George S. Kaufman, and Stephen Sondheim, who occasionally drops in on weekends.

A full country breakfast served by congenial host and inkeeper Mary

Schnitzer in the main dining room adds to a visit. Schnitzer will gladly offer details of Hammerstein's life in the house. The Highland Farms' serene setting atop a hill is a fitting tribute to Hammerstein, who was inspired to write so many great lyrics from this setting.

Highland Farms

ACCOMMODATIONS: Five-room bed-and-breakfast

DIRECTIONS: From Philadelphia stay on I-95 north to Route 332 west for 3.7 miles. Get on Route 413 north for 10.4 miles to Route 202 south to Doylestown. After about 10 miles you will come to an intersection; take the second left onto East Road. Highland Farms is the fourth house on the right.

The Mansion Inn

Bucks County's only AAA Four-Diamond inn is one of the most luxurious in the area. The splendidly restored Victorian inn, one of the few remaining in the area, has eight rooms for guests and a newly added restaurant. The Ashby suite, along with the Balmoral suite, recalls the English influence with four-poster beds and period antiques. The Warwick suite and Kensington suites are among the inn's largest accommodations.

A handsome collection of antique clocks is found throughout the inn, which reminds one more of a very fine house than an inn. Guests can enjoy French toast or the Mansion egg dish *du jour* at breakfast. All of the pastries and baked goods are made on the premises, and the restaurant features a selection of American and European dishes and delights.

Cozy luxury found at the Mansion Inn greets visitors to the former Victorian home in the heart of Bucks County. *The Mansion Inn*

9 South Main Street
New Hope, PA 18938
Tel: (215) 862-1231
www.themansioninn.com
$$$$
158 miles/3¼ hours

ACCOMMODATIONS: Eight-room bed-and-breakfast

DIRECTIONS: Take I-95 north past central Philadelphia to Exit 51 to New Hope (Route 32 north) You will see the Mansion Inn on your left. Turn left at the traffic light (Bridge Street, or Route 179). The parking entrance is on your left.

Excursions & Diversions

With its origins as an artists' colony, Bucks County is endowed with two unique art enclaves. So following your country drives, antique shopping, and afternoon tea in a rustic tavern, head out to the Pearl Buck House and the James Michener Art Museum for a taste of all that this area has to offer.

The visual artists paved the way for the literary ones, with painters Edward Redfield and William Lathrop leading the way for the writers and songwriters who staked their claim here in the 1930s, '40s, and '50s. Dorothy Parker, George S. Kaufman, Moss Hart, Oscar Hammerstein, and S. J. Perelman bought homes in the area on their "creative retreats" from New York City.

The glamorous era remains today with the Pearl S. Buck House and James Michener Art Museum providing key insights into Bucks County's history as a wellspring of talent.

The Pearl S. Buck House reveals the legacy of author, activist, and humanitarian Pearl Buck, whose 1835 farmhouse is open to the public.

Following her years in China, Buck purchased the farmhouse in 1934, naming it Green Hills Farm. On the National Register of Historic Places, the house is open year round for special events, art exhibits, and the Spring Craft Festival held in March. The event features dozens of regional artists and their crafts.

One can tour the home year round, with the holiday season the most beautiful time to tour. Garlands, an ornately decorated Christmas tree, and carolers add to the holiday festivities. Pearl Buck International Day is a multifamily festival event offering games and cultural entertainment.

Located ten minutes from Doylestown, the home is open for tours Tuesday through Saturday at 11 a.m., 1 p.m., and 2 p.m. and Sundays at 1 p.m. and 2 p.m. The grounds are closed Mondays and major holidays and during January and February. For further information contact 1-800-220-2825, ext 170, (215) 249-0100.

Named after Doylestown's Pulitzer Prize–winning author, the James Michener Art Museum opened in 1988 to vividly display and showcase the cultural contributions of the Bucks County region.

Within the striking and unusual complex one can find an intimate exhibition celebrating the life and works of Michener. The writer's Bucks County office is on view along with his Presidential Medal of Freedom and the original manuscript of "the Novel," as the museum calls it.

The Lenfest Exhibition showcases the works of Bucks County painters including Edward Redfield and George Sotter. The collection, a gift from the private holdings of Marguerite and Gerry Lenfest, tells the story of the New Hope artists' colony.

The Creative Bucks County Gallery is particularly appealing to literary buffs. A multimedia interactive exhibit studies the accomplishments of many artists, authors, playwrights, lyricists, and composers who have lived in the area. A host of talents is explored in this gallery, including Pearl S. Buck, Oscar Hammerstein, Moss Hart, George S. Kaufman, and S. J. Perelman among others.

Other highlights within the museum include the Garber Mural, a twenty-two-foot mural by painter Daniel Garner done in 1926, which originally appeared in the Sesquicentennial Exhibition in Philadelphia, and the visual heritage of Bucks County detailing both the impressionists and modernists of Bucks County.

The Bucks County Convention and Visitors Bureau

3207 Street Road
Bensalem, PA 19020
Tel: 1-800-836-BUCKS; (215) 639-0300
www.buckscountycvb.org

GETTYSBURG

The Gettysburg Hotel

Mention the word Gettysburg and thoughts of the nation's most famous Civil War battlefield come to mind. A scenic and comfortable 1½-hour drive from Washington makes the Pennsylvania town an ideal weekend getaway for travelers seeking to explore the details surrounding the July 4, 1863, conflict. The life of former president Dwight D. Eisenhower, who settled in Gettysburg following his White House years, can also be explored on a visit.

Historic plaque and cannons at the site of the battle of Gettysburg. *Steve Foxwell*

One Lincoln Square
Gettysburg, PA 17325
Tel: (717) 337-2000
Tel. 1-800-528-1234
**   (Best Western)**
www.gettysburg-hotel.com
$$$
78 miles/1½ hours

Both of these sites are within easy reach of one another and highlight different facets of the Civil War town.

Established in 1797 when James Scott opened a tavern, the hotel became a backdrop in the summer of 1863 during the bloody three-day Battle of Gettysburg, which forever changed the town's and the nation's history. Located at One Lincoln Square in the heart of the historic district, the Best Western property is ideal for Civil War buffs wanting to explore the many historical aspects of Gettysburg.

A member of the National Trusts Historic Hotels group, the Hotel Gettysburg is of paramount significance. Across the street, the Wills House, where President Abraham Lincoln completed the Gettysburg Address, displays its own rich history.

President Lincoln is not the only president to be associated with the hotel. Dwight Eisenhower first visited the Hotel Gettysburg in 1915 while a young cadet at West Point, only to return in 1918 when he was assigned his first command at Camp Colt. Eisenhower spent his first four nights at the hotel, a stay about which he fondly reminisced in his later years. From his early visits Eisenhower eventually decided to buy a farm and settle in Gettysburg, a place that had become so dear to his heart.

During Eisenhower's presidency he often visited the hotel when he stayed at his farm. At the height of the Cold War Eisenhower used the hotel as a national operations center. Both Lincoln and Eisenhower saw the hotel as a peaceful enclave amidst the immense pressures of their presidencies. A long list of luminaries and historical figures can be found in the hotel's annals, including Daniel Webster who visited in 1833, William Henry Harrison, Francis Scott Key, Gen. Ulysses S. Grant, and Frederick Douglass. The poet Carl Sandburg's name is also found among its list of former guests. Sandburg stayed at the hotel while writing a portion of his biography of Abraham Lincoln.

In 1925 Lt. George Pickett, third grandson of Gen. George Pickett, who led Pickett's Charge at Gettysburg, stayed at the hotel. Three years later golfing great Bobby Jones made an appearance. Other names of note include Gen. George Marshall, Gen. Omar Bradley, Mrs. Woodrow Wilson, and auto magnate Henry Ford, who visited in 1934.

Sen. Barry Goldwater attended a dinner at the hotel with the Eisenhowers on December 14, 1964—the date the hotel closed its doors.

Several years later the hotel reopened and underwent a series of transformations and renovations during which its 105 guest rooms were remodeled along with its richly appointed lobby with its wood-burning fireplace. The Lincoln Dining Room was also spruced up with new carpets and drapers recalling the flavor of its eighteenth-century décor.

The historic hallmark hotel's setting in the lovely town of Gettysburg adds to a visit. It continues to host luminaries including David and Julie Eisenhower, who live in the area.

Best Western Gettysburg Hotel

ACCOMMODATIONS: A Best Western Hotel; eighty-three guest rooms and twenty-two suites. Swimming pool.

DIRECTIONS: The hotel is located at One Lincoln Square at the junction of Route 30 and Business Route 15. Approximately 1½ hour's drive from Washington. From the Washington beltway (I-495) take 270 north to Route 15 west through Frederick, Maryland, to Gettysburg.

Excursions & Diversions

The Gettysburg National Military Park and the Eisenhower Home are the historical highlights in Gettysburg. Plan on spending at least two to three days in Gettysburg in order to have plenty of time to for exploring these diverse and historically significant sites.

The Gettysburg National Military Park was the location of the largest Civil War battle. The battle began on July 1, 1863, and ended three days later with the climactic Pickett's Charge proclaiming the Union victory.

Open year round, the park has a comprehensive visitors center south of Gettysburg between Route 134 and Business Route 15. Open daily from 8 a.m. until 5 p.m., the center is closed on major holidays. The electric map accurately presents an ideal orientation to all there is to see in the park.

Touring the park is best done by taking a self-guided driving tour with an audio tour that can be rented or purchased through the gift shop, or by hiring a licensed battlefield guide for a more comprehensive tour. Allow at least two hours for the self-guided tour. If you choose to tour with a licensed battlefield guide, the visitors center will arrange the tour. The guide's fee depends on the number of people in your group.

Plans are under way at press time to open a new museum and visitors center at Gettysburg. The new structure, to be built under a cooperative agreement between the National Park Service and the Gettysburg National Battlefield Museum Foundation, will orient visitors to both the town and the park. It will house exhibits on the Civil War and feature Civil War and Gettysburg artifacts. The proposed $95 million project will also house a new amphitheater for evening and educational programs.

Gettysburg Convention and Visitors Bureau

35 Carlisle Street
Gettysburg, PA 17325
Tel: (717) 334-6274
www.gettysburg.com

HERSHEY

The Hotel Hershey

America's most famous and renowned chocolatier, Milton Hershey, also founded one of the country's most historic hotels. The Hotel Hershey proves inviting for those with a sweet tooth or for travelers seeking to explore America's most famous chocolate empire.

The elaborate Fountain Lobby with its Italian motif greets guests to the Mobil Four-Star Hotel Hershey. *The Hotel Hershey*

There is no escaping the magic of Hershey's chocolate on a visit here where the streetlights are in the shape of Hershey kisses and the aroma of chocolate wafts through the air.

The town, founded by Hershey in 1903, revolves around all things chocolate. In fact, everything of importance in Hershey is named after Hershey. Hershey Park, Hershey Gardens, and the Hershey Museum are a few of the town's sites named after

**PO Box 4001 Hotel Road
Hershey, PA 17033-0400
Tel: (717) 533-2171
1-800-HERSHEY
www.hersheyresorts.com
$$$$
150 miles/2¼ hours**

the town's richest and greatest benefactor. Hershey's Chocolate World is the official visitors center of Hershey Foods and an ideal starting point on a Hershey exploration.

But it is the grandeur found at the Hershey Hotel that best personifies the town's most important and most visited architectural landmark.

A native Pennsylvanian, Hershey, who only completed the fourth grade, learned the candy business in nearby Lancaster, where in 1883 the fledgling twenty-four-year-old entrepreneur established the Lancaster Caramel Company. An instant success, Hershey became fascinated with the art of making chocolate at the 1893 World's Columbian Exposition and three years after attending the event sold his caramel business to concentrate on chocolate.

The delicious taste of milk chocolate intrigued him from the beginning. Hershey was determined to develop a milk chocolate equal to the exacting standards of the Swiss. In 1903 he fulfilled his long-awaited dream when he built a mass-production facility for making milk chocolate. With his success in chocolate came the inspiration for building a grand new hotel. A new hotel would not only add new jobs and improve Hershey's economic situation, but would also attract visitors to the area. Building the hotel in 1933, at the height of the Great Depression, did not deter Hershey from constructing the grandest hotel the area had ever seen. The 235-room hotel bearing Hershey's name is a member of the Historic Hotels of America and Preferred Hotels. It has earned the status ranking of an AAA Four-Diamond hotel. A grand-opening banquet was held opening weekend for the hotel on May 23, 1933.

Journalist Lowell Thomas once said that the "Hotel Hershey is a palace that out palaces the maharajas of India." His statement aptly applies today. The ornate Fountain Lobby was completely renovated and refurbished in 1998. The azure-blue cloud ceiling has been beautifully repainted, and the floor tiles, after decades of wax buildup, have been stripped to their original luster. The Circular Dining Room, one of Hershey's most ambitious projects, displays thirteen expansive windows surrounding guests as they dine. The Mediterranean flavor that Hershey envisioned has been implemented throughout the stately property, complete with mosaic tiles, wooden balustrades, and lavish fountains.

During its reign as one of Pennsylvania's finest hotels, the Hershey has witnessed a stream of celebrated guests. On January 30, 1935, a second nationwide birthday ball was held for President Franklin Roosevelt to raise funds for infantile paralysis. Other famous guests throughout its history have included Dwight Eisenhower, Bob Hope, Rose Kennedy, golfer Ben Hogan, Frank Sinatra, and cowboy star Gene Autry. The great grandson of Charles Dickens, Gerald Charles Dickens, gave a reading of *A Christmas Carol* at two hotel events in December 1998. Olympic hopefuls and many Hollywood names have also graced its annals.

During World War II, Hershey made significant contributions to the war effort. He devoted much of his bulk-chocolate production to the military and developed the Ration D bar, a survival ration chocolate bar for soldiers facing extreme conditions. The hotel's many amenities include a wide range of diversions. Tennis courts, golf, indoor/outdoor swimming pools, and a variety of chocolate-themed restaurants and gift shops make a visit a complete experience.

The Cocoa Beanery is a perennial favorite where delectable hot chocolate Hershey-style along with baked goods is on the menu. Gourmet teas and coffees can be purchased in the attractive eatery.

The newest and splashiest addition is the opulent Hershey Spa, with interior design based on Hershey's mansion at High Point. A replica of a stained-glass window from his home, accented by gleaming hardwood floors, makes for a grand entrance.

Activities abound at the hotel. Kite flying, bike rentals, cross-country skiing, and romantic carriage rides are just a few of the outings the visitor can enjoy while staying here.

The Hotel Hershey

ACCOMMODATIONS: 235 guest rooms, 4 dining rooms, room service, fitness center and spa, tennis courts, and meeting facilities. Complimentary transportation to local attractions and free admission to Hershey Park and Museum.

DIRECTIONS: From I-495 follow Route 270 north to Frederick and follow to Route 15 north; go on Route 15 north, to 581 east, to I-83 north toward Harrisburg, I-83 north to 322 east. Follow 322 east into Hershey.

Excursions & Diversions

There is no escaping the world of chocolate in Hershey. Hershey Park and Hershey's Chocolate World are two sidelights. Hershey Park, an easy-to-get-around theme park, offers rides and amusements for children. Gift shops abound with Hershey's chocolates, so prepare to be tempted on this adventure. Chocolate World presents a simulated tour of the Hershey Chocolate Factory where you will go behind the scenes and learn the secrets of chocolate making. At the end of this tour a free sample is offered to all who enter. This is also where devotees of Hershey's chocolate can find everything imaginable in the way of gifts with the Hershey logo.

The Hershey Theatre is the cultural venue. Located in downtown Hershey, this magnificent performing arts center stages Broadway shows, classical musical concerts, and dance attractions. The Hershey Museum is a great place for learning more about the legacy of Milton Hershey. Photographs, exhibits, and artifacts detailing life in early Hershey can also be found here.

www.hersheypa.com
Tel: 1-800-Hershey (1-800-437-7439)
100 West Hershey Park Drive
Hershey, PA 17033

PHILADELPHIA
The Park Hyatt Philadelphia at the Bellevue

Philadelphia, approximately a two-hour drive from Washington, is the state's cultural center and hometown to actress Grace Kelly, who fondly remembered her hometown long after her marriage to Prince Rainier of Monaco. At night a string of lights outlines Boathouse Row where many rowers, including Kelly's brother, Jack, have carved out their dreams. Philadelphia is also the city where the Oscar-winning movie *Rocky* was filmed. It boasts one of the largest outdoor sculpture gardens of Rodin's work outside Paris.

The City of Brotherly Love is most famous for being the place where the Declaration of Independence was signed and the Constitution was drafted. Fairmount Park, its lush urban oasis encompassing 8,579 acres, is to Philadelphians what Central Park is to New Yorkers. Miles upon miles of green space overlooking the winding Schuylkill River offer scenic drives, walks, and unspoiled bridle trails for residents and visitors alike.

Within this beautiful city three distinctly different but outstanding lodging establishments offer Philadelphia's best. The Park Hyatt Philadelphia at the Bellevue, the Latham, and the Independence Park Hotel are the recommended choices for travelers seeking out genuine pieces of Philadelphia's history.

The Park Hyatt displays by far the most storied history of the group. Centrally located in Center City and near all of the familiar landmarks, the fully

The elegant lobby of the Park Hyatt Philadelphia at the Bellevue.

Broad Street between Walnut and Locust Streets
1415 Chancellor Court
Philadelphia, PA 19102
Tel: (215) 893-1234
1-800-233-1234
www.hyatt.com
$$$$
143 miles/approximately two hours

restored 1904 National Historic Landmark is a Mobil Four-Star and AAA Four-Diamond hotel.

Within its walls portions of Philadelphia's history come to life. Entering its portals is similar to stepping inside a fine art museum. A favorite of the actress Ethel Barrymore, who often stayed in the original Bellevue Hotel, it reveals many layers of history.

Although associated with Hyatt Hotels, the hotel, originally called the Bellevue Hotel, has not lost its distinctive characteristics and flavor that vividly recall the Gilded Age. Its founder and primary architect, George Charles Boldt, often referred to as the "father of the modern American hotel," sculpted an original when he envisioned the Bellevue. Today the Park Hyatt continues to be the city's most beautiful and historic hotel, offering a genuine taste of "old Philadelphia" while keeping up with the times and offering guests all of the amenities of a first-class luxury hotel.

Boldt, who settled in Philadelphia to learn the hotel business, was an Irish immigrant who came to the city with very little money but an abundance of dreams. Working his way up from bellman to front-desk manager at a variety of hotels and lodging establishments in the city, Boldt quickly learned that to attract the carriage trade he had to offer the best of everything with service being at the top of the list.

After saving money and attracting investors, Boldt decided to launch out on his own in 1881 and built his own hotel, which resembled a club more than a hotel. Boldt put his plan into motion by implementing all of the amenities associated with the great European hotels. His attention to detail and superb service quickly became the talk of the town, where he successfully carved out a reputation as one of the Philadelphia's best hoteliers attracting the city's social elite.

Forming the Clover Club, a private gentlemen's dining club within the hotel, Boldt attracted a colorful array of stage actors and visiting celebrities including Samuel Clemens (Mark Twain), who attended a dinner at the hotel in April 1885. The dinner attended by Twain was only one of several events that set the stage for the Bellevue's becoming Philadelphia's choice lodging address. During the dinner that Twain attended, an actor by the name of Edwin Booth, who was performing in the city, sat next to the humorist. While the nature of their conversation is not known, it is believed that the dinner party was a lively and entertaining event.

During the next twenty years the Clover Club would host every U.S. president with the exception of Theodore Roosevelt. In addition to attracting the rich and powerful men of the Gilded Age, the Bellevue also became renowned for its balls, receptions, and endless social events for Philadelphia society.

In 1888, seven years after the Bellevue Hotel opened, Boldt purchased the property across the street—a site that would eventually become the nineteen-story, mansard-roofed Bellevue-Stratford Hotel.

Sixteen years later, the Bellevue-Stratford opened to the public with great fanfare in Philadelphia. Costing close to $5 million, the hotel displayed every luxury and comfort. Marble bathrooms, Oriental carpets, priceless paintings, and valuable artifacts adorned the hotel's opulent interior.

The Bellevue-Stratford's official opening occurred at one minute past midnight on September 19, 1904, and was attended by society *grandes dames*, European aristocracy, and dignitaries. Tall marble columns rising to the ornate coffered and gilded ceiling, a grand circular staircase embellished with wrought-iron railings, and rare art treasures gathered from around the globe reflected the opulence of the Gilded Age.

The Bellevue-Stratford was a resounding hit from the beginning, attracting the likes of New York millionaire John Jacob Astor, who was so impressed with Boldt's skills as a hotelier that he later employed him to manage his own Waldorf-Astoria.

The Palm Garden, the Viennese Tea Room, and the guest rooms, completely furnished by Philadelphia merchant John Wanamaker, added to the hotel's mystique and charm. During the 1920s the Bellevue-Stratford flourished as Philadelphia's most preferred and palatial hotel. Attracting stage actors and statesmen, the Bellevue continued its reign as the city's most luxurious hotel. It is rumored that author Bram Stoker wrote part of *Dracula* while staying at the hotel, and before her marriage to Prince Rainier of Monaco, Philadelphia beauty Grace Kelly attended many social functions at the Bellevue.

But not all of the hotel's chapters have been happy ones. Tragedy struck in July 1976 when several hundred American Legion members became ill at the hotel. The South Cameo Room, where the group dined, became infected with airborne bacteria, which caused an illness now referred to as legionnaires' disease. Twenty-nine people were struck down by the deadly disease, and as a result, the old Bellevue-Stratford's reputation was tarnished, some thought forever.

When the hotel closed its doors on October 7, 1976, thoughts around the city were that the "grande dame of Philadelphia hotels" would never be the same. For two years the beloved landmark lay dormant, and there was even talk of tearing the building down. With the determined efforts of Dr. George Thomas, a Philadelphia art historian, the revered and treasured landmark was saved from the wrecking ball. Owing to Thomas's efforts, the hotel was placed on the National Register of Historic Places and a new era began for the Bellevue-Stratford, and with it a piece of Philadelphia history was saved.

Because of the conscientious efforts of Ronald Rubin, a successful Philadelphia real estate businessman who bought the hotel for over $8 million, hopes were restored of renovating the fading architectural beauty that had become such an integral part of Philadelphia.

It was during the reign of the Fairmont Group, the first onboard in managing the mammoth property, that extensive renovations began. Philadelphia architect Hyman Myers supervised the monumental task of restoring the beauty of the once grand hotel. All of the original marble was cleaned and polished, and costly modernizations were put in place throughout the hotel.

By 1979, the Bellevue-Stratford had been completely restored. Eventually Westin Hotels managed the property, then Cunard, and finally Hyatt Hotels, which presently manages the stately structure.

Another $100 million was spent ten years later to add the masterful French Renaissance touches that remain throughout today. Guests are quickly transported from the hotel's street-level entrance to the nineteenth-floor lobby. The hotel's most striking room is the Ethel Barrymore Room, where massive domes and Palladian windows accent afternoon tea.

Named after one of its famous early guests, the oval-shaped room is the hotel's architectural showpiece, with its exquisite, hand-painted, pastel dome ceiling and exceptional birds-eye views of Philadelphia.

In addition, the Philadelphia Library Room, also on the nineteenth floor, displays the ambience of an English gentleman's club with its dark woods and working fireplace. An outstanding collection of books by or about noted Philadelphians can also be found here.

All of the hotel's 172 guest rooms are designed in American Empire style, and the seven-story Garden Conservatory is reminiscent of the hotel's Gilded Age.

Another treat in store is the collection of fine shops located on the first three levels of the building. Here you can find Tiffany & Co., Polo/Ralph Lauren, Nicole Miller, and Williams-Sonoma. The Palm Restaurant, a steak and seafood restaurant, is also within this dazzling shopping arcade.

Park Hyatt Philadelphia at the Bellevue

ACCOMMODATIONS: An elegant city hotel with 130 newly renovated rooms, four restaurants, health club and pool, day spa, and salon.

DIRECTIONS: Follow I-95 north into the heart of Center City and take the Broad Street/Route 611 exit. The hotel is located approximately 2.5 miles up Broad Street on the left between Locust and Walnut Streets. You will need to enter the center lane to make a left either into the garage or Chancellor Court. Fee for overnight parking.

𝒯𝒽𝑒 𝐵𝑒𝓈𝓉 𝒲𝑒𝓈𝓉𝑒𝓇𝓃 𝐼𝓃𝒹𝑒𝓅𝑒𝓃𝒹𝑒𝓃𝒸𝑒 𝒫𝒶𝓇𝓀 𝐻𝑜𝓉𝑒𝓁

Often referred to as "Philadelphia's great little hotel," the Independence Park is a tiny treasure in the heart of the historic district. Ideally situated one block from Independence Hall, this hotel is accessible to all of the major sights and unbeatable for families desiring a quality economical hotel.

The sister property of the Gettysburg Hotel, the Independence Park was originally a dry goods store designed by Philadelphia architect Joseph Hoxie in 1856 and is the only small hotel whose architecture predates the Civil War. Its grand staircase, high ceilings, and thirty-six designer-appointed guest rooms beautifully blend together in making this little hotel one of the city's best-kept secrets.

Just steps away from the Liberty Bell is the Independence Park Hotel. *Independence Park Hotel*

Listed on the National Register of Historic Places, the Independence Park sits on the fringes of Society Hill where a host of dining options is available. In addition to its proximity to Independence Hall, the hotel is within easy reach of Elfreth's Alley and the Betsy Ross House.

A colonial décor prevails throughout the inn, which resembles a townhouse where

235 Chestnut Street
Philadelphia, PA 19106
Tel: (215) 922-4443,
1-800-624-2988
www.independence
parkhotel.com
$$
143 miles/3 hours

personal touches are its most memorable feature. A complimentary European-style breakfast is included in the room tariff, as are afternoon tea and snacks and a weekly fireside wine and cheese reception.

It is the exceptional service found at the Independence Park that separates this very fine boutique hotel from others in the city. The unique Bourse Shopping area and Society Hill are just steps away from the hotel's front door.

The combination of affordable price with understated elegance makes this gem of a hotel an ideal lodging spot for families.

The Independence Park Hotel

ACCOMMODATIONS: A Best Western Hotel. Complimentary European breakfast.

DIRECTIONS: Follow I-95 north into Center City Philadelphia and take Exit 22. Follow signs for Independence Hall and turn left onto Fourth Street, then make a quick left onto Chestnut Street. The hotel is on the left side between Second and Third Streets.

The Latham Hotel

In 1907 the story of the Latham began. On the site of the present hotel was the former home of William Bucknell, philanthropist and founder of Bucknell University.

Eight years later the fourteen-story structure opened its doors as the Latham Apartment House, quickly becoming one of the city's choicest and most desirable addresses. It was not until 1960 that a group of Philadelphia investors decided to transform the apartment into a luxury hotel. Ten years later the hotel officially opened, and today it remains one of the city's loveliest smaller hotels.

Modeled along the lines of a fine European-style hotel, the Latham is an intimate place to hang your hat while in Philadelphia. Its location near all of the major sights and in one of the city's most beautiful neighborhoods makes the Latham a continuing favorite for discerning travelers.

A major restoration and renovation took place in 1997; many of the guest rooms and public areas were remodeled to

The doorway of the luxurious Latham Hotel near Rittenhouse Square in Philadelphia. *The Latham Hotel*

135 South Seventeenth Street
Philadelphia, PA 19103
Tel: (215) 563-7474;
  1-877-Latham-1
  (1-877-528-4261)
www.lathamhotel.com
$$$
144 miles/3 hours

resemble a very fine townhouse. Period antiques and art found in its guest rooms add the personal touches often missing from the larger hotel chains.

Being so close to Rittenhouse Square and an array of the city's most beautiful shops has made the Latham the discreet choice of a host of celebrities and dignitaries over the years. Just ask Joe Broderick, its thirty-two-year-veteran doorman, who will gladly expound on the Latham's storied history.

The hotel offers 139 guest rooms, all designed with an upscale Colonial décor. Jolly's Grillroom is the place to be on Friday and Saturday evenings. Fresh seafood and steaks are the order of the day at Jolly's, which is a favorite of the city's politicos and visiting celebrities. During the Army-Navy game, usually held the weekend after Thanksgiving, be sure and book well in advance, as Navy fans take over the Latham!

The Latham Hotel

ACCOMMODATIONS: European-style boutique hotel with 139 rooms. Restaurant.

DIRECTIONS: Follow I-95 north into Center City, Philadelphia, and get off at Seventeenth Street near Independence Hall and the Liberty Bell Pavilion. The hotel is located one block from Liberty Place shopping and dining.

Excursions & Diversions

Philadelphia's compact size and efficient public transportation make it an easy city to explore. Walking is the best way to get to know Philly's neighborhoods and sites. Purchasing a City Pass through the Philadelphia Convention and Visitors Bureau is the most economical way of seeing the most sites; it gives admission to the Franklin Institute Science Museum, the Academy of Natural Sciences, the Philadelphia Zoo, the Philly Trolley Tour, and the Independence Seaport Museum.

The city is a great mix of old and new architecture, with Independence Hall, the Bourse, Society Hill and Penn's Landing, and the Philadelphia Museum of Art the most interesting areas to explore.

Independence Hall, between Fifth and Sixth Streets on Chestnut, is the city's most important and most visited historical landmark. The 1732 building was the location of the Second Continental Congress, and both the Declaration of Independence and Constitution were signed there.

It is also where Gen. George Washington accepted the post of commander in chief for the Colonial armies. The Assembly Room displays the chair that Washington sat in during the drafting of the Constitution and the inkstand used in the signing of the Declaration of Independence.

The new Liberty Bell Center in Independence National Historical Park at Market and 6th Streets is another of the city's historical highlights. National Park rangers give talks on the history of the Liberty Bell and its significance in the American story.

Also within this area is the Bourse, Philadelphia's most historic shopping emporium. The Bourse, former location of the Philadelphia Stock Exchange, is filled with unusual shops and eateries and is recommended for a stop following your Independence Hall and Liberty Bell tours.

Museums are plentiful in the City of Brotherly Love. The exceptional ones include the Rodin Museum, which houses and displays a 124-piece collection of the master sculptor—the largest outside Paris—and the Philadelphia Museum of Art. Founded in 1876, the museum ranks among the world's best with its priceless collection of prints and oil paintings. The Thomas Eakins collection is the largest collection devoted to the painter in the country and the museum's most treasured.

Other painters represented in the museum include Paul Cézanne, Claude Monet, Pierre-Auguste Renoir, and Vincent van Gogh.

For children the Franklin Institute Science Museum is a colorful hands-on museum exhibiting the wonders of science. A national memorial to Benjamin Franklin, the museum contains exhibits that demonstrate many of Franklin's ideas and displays many of his personal effects.

Philadelphia Convention and Visitors Bureau

1515 Market Street
Suite 2020
Philadelphia, PA 19102
Tel: (215) 636-3300
www.pcvb.org

YORK
The Yorktowne Hotel

Music greats, Eleanor Roosevelt, and Clinton/Gore's first campaign stop in 1992 have put the Yorktowne Hotel on the map.

York, the nation's capital during the Revolutionary War when Philadelphia was under the British and mapped out by William Penn, is a meticulously restored historic destination worthy of a weekend excursion.

The Yorktowne Hotel, a AAA Three-Diamond hotel, sits in the center of the historic district on Market Street. Its easy accessibility to a variety of other historic towns—Gettysburg twenty-nine miles to the east and Lancaster County twenty-four miles to the west—makes York an ideal launching point for reaching an array of diverse Pennsylvania locations.

The lovely and inviting Yorktowne Hotel sits in the center of York's historic district. *Yorktowne Hotel*

48 East Market Street
York, PA 17401
Tel: 1-800-233-9324;
(717) 848-1111
www.yorktowne.com
$$
100 miles/2 hours

The hotel's importance to York can be traced back to the early 1920s, when the Chamber of Commerce decided to build a "community hotel." Residents of York became stockholders of the hotel, allowing it to open debt free. Costing over $1 million, the hotel opened to great fanfare on October 17, 1925, with opening reviews billing it as the "best hotel between New York and Pittsburgh."

The eleven-story Renaissance Revival hotel reveals touches borrowed from the Art Deco period with its twenty-foot-high ceilings, shimmering brass and crystal chandeliers, and intricate moldings in its public spaces. The 120 guest rooms, revamped and redecorated in 1998, display bright floral prints and pastel chintz fabrics, antique reproductions, and marble tile baths. The Commonwealth Room, its award-winning AAA Four-Diamond restaurant, specializes in American and European cuisine. The Grand Ballroom recalls and recaptures the Yorktowne's bygone era with its polished oak floors and sparkling chandeliers.

Its guest roster includes many music legends who have performed at the nearby Strand-Capital Performing Arts Center. Ella Fitzgerald, Henry Mancini, Count Basie, Tony Bennett, Tommy Dorsey, Duke Ellington, Marvin Hamlisch, and Benny Goodman were former guests. Bob Hope, First Lady Eleanor Roosevelt, Hedy Lamar, and Ozzie and Harriett Nelson's names can also be added to the stellar list.

In July 1992 Governor Bill Clinton of Arkansas and Senator Al Gore of Tennessee kicked off the first phase of their presidential campaign at the Yorktowne. The candidates began an extensive "whistle-stop" bus tour across the United States from the Yorktowne.

The Yorktowne's amenities include a van service pickup (fee) from the Harrisburg Airport and Amtrak's rail station, complimentary valet parking for patrons of the hotel and restaurant, and a health and fitness center.

The Yorktowne Hotel

ACCOMMODATIONS: 120 guestrooms, two restaurants, fitness center, free valet parking.

DIRECTIONS: From Washington beltway take Route I-95 north to I-695 (Baltimore beltway) west to I-83 north. Follow I-83 north to Exit 15 to South George Street north of King Street. Turn onto King Street and go one block to Duke Street. Turn left onto Duke Street. The Yorktowne Hotel garage is a half block on the left.

Excursions & Diversions

With its orderly street patterns ingeniously laid out by William Penn's surveyors, York serves up a host of historic walking tours where more than thirty-four restored eighteenth-, nineteenth-, and twentieth-century structures can be explored. The Golden Plough Tavern, built in 1741, is the oldest building in York; other old taverns include the Gates and the Golden Swan.

The "Murals of York" are one of York's most distinctive features. Twenty larger-than-life, colorful murals along Cherry Lane highlight various periods

---

in the city's history from Colonial times to the Great Depression and World War II. Started in 1996, the murals project artfully showcases York's history through illustrated panels.

Some murals to look out for include *York in the 1800s* at 237 West Market Street and the *Harley-Davidson Tradition* at 258 West Market. In the Harley-Davidson motorcycle mural, Arthur Davidson, one of the company's founders, is seen astride an early Harley with the background detailing a 1950s factory scene. The Harley-Davidson plant is open for tours Monday through Friday. The Pfaltzgraff Pottery showroom and factory is another recommended side trip. Visitors can see the shaping and molding of pottery objects made by the Pennsylvania company.

Often referred as the "snack capital of the world," because so many snacks are made and shipped from here, York offers tours through many of these interesting venues for food aficionados.

For outdoor recreation York County offers three state parks, four lakes, and a ski area. Bird watching, hiking, and biking can all be enjoyed within an easy ride from the downtown area, with Ski Roundtop the place to go for skiing and snowboarding. The Heritage Trail is a great spot for exploring the outdoor areas near York. Beginning at the Colonial Courthouse and stretching for twenty-one miles to the Maryland border, the rail trail is one of the easiest to navigate in Pennsylvania.

York County Convention and Visitors Bureau

Tel: 1-888-858-YORK (9675)
www.yorkpa.org

CHAPTER 2 *Delaware*

WILMINGTON
Hotel du Pont

The Brandywine River Valley recalls a Currier and Ives painting where rustic country inns, fieldstone houses, and fences that stretch for miles can be enjoyed on a visit. A "Wyeth painting" might be a better description of the bucolic landscape that has inspired three generations of Wyeths.

The Brandywine area, where southeastern Pennsylvania meets Delaware, is du Pont and Wyeth country. Two of America's most important legacies and dynasties, the Wyeths and the du Ponts, can be studied while exploring Brandywine's rich repository of museums set amidst a pastoral landscape.

The beautiful paintings of the Wyeth family accent the famed Brandywine Room at the Hotel du Pont. *Hotel duPont*

Eleventh and Market Streets
Wilmington, DE 19801
Tel: (302) 594-3100,
**   1-800-441-9019**
www.hoteldupont.com
$$$$
135 miles/2½ hours

While the du Pont family settled in Wilmington making their initial fortune with the gunpowder mills, the Wyeths, N. C., Andrew, and Jamie, became inspired by the beauty of the Brandywine to create their master paintings, illustrations, sketches, and drawings, ultimately becoming America's premier artistic family.

Millionaires can dare to dream without limits, and Pierre du Pont did just that by envisioning and eventually building Wilmington's Hotel du Pont. Realizing Wilmington's strategic location between the capital of commerce, New York, and the power brokers of Washington, du Pont planned the Hotel du Pont.

Situated in the center of downtown Wilmington, the du Pont with its ornate European design complements the countryside setting of the Inn at Montchanin—both du Pont creations and Wilmington's most historic accommodations. Both of these unique properties offer the best that Wilmington and the Brandywine has to offer.

The Hotel du Pont, opened January 15, 1913, is just blocks away from the

Amtrak station with New York and Washington connections. Owned and operated by the DuPont Company, the hotel, a Mobil Four-Star, AAA Four-Diamond hotel, displays Italian Renaissance architecture in its public areas. All of the hotels' 206 rooms and 11 suites were renovated in 1992 at a cost of $40 million. Plush earth-tone interiors accent its guest rooms that offer all of the amenities one associates with a AAA Four-Diamond property.

The Green Room, its formal no-holds-barred dining room, recalls the grand palaces of Europe with its Italian mosaic foyer and oak beams in the embellished coffered ceiling. The hotel's more intimate dining venue, the Brandywine Room, displays original paintings by the Wyeth family on its wine-colored walls. The famous brush strokes of NC., Jamie, and Andrew make dining here similar to being served in an art gallery. The Brandywine Room is a favorite of visiting celebrities, including actors Gregory Peck and Ingrid Bergman, who preferred the room's low-key atmosphere and soft-lit interiors while in residence.

The hotel's guest list is peppered with the names of baseball greats, presidents, captains of industry, and Hollywood stars. The Yankee Clipper, Joe DiMaggio, was a former guest, as were Admiral Bull Halsey and playwright Eugene O'Neill. Charles Lindbergh, Amelia Earhart, Gene Autry, Tommy Dorsey, Oscar Hammerstein, and tennis great Bill Tilden were all guests at the Du Pont.

When actress Rosalind Russell was in town performing *Auntie Mame* at the adjoining Playhouse Theatre, she received a standing ovation upon entering the Green Room following a performance rivaling the ovation given aviator Charles Lindbergh, who had been a guest at the hotel several years earlier.

The Du Pont offers a variety of packages throughout the year with the Yuletide season proving one of the more popular. Most packages include admission to the area's major attractions and sites including the Brandywine River Museum, Winterthur, and Longwood Gardens.

The theater at the Du Pont has played a key role in attracting top talent to the region. Adjoining the hotel, the playhouse is another architectural landmark worth visiting while in Wilmington. The playhouse, operated by a series of owners since its opening night on October 15, 1913, is a highlight at the Du Pont, where such acting greats as Katharine Hepburn, Henry Fonda, Helen Hayes, Lionel Barrymore, Mae West, Al Jolson, and Bette Davis have graced its stages. Photographs of the famous actors outline the entrance to the theater, which continues to host some of Broadway's brightest.

Hotel du Pont

ACCOMMODATIONS: Elegant European-style hotel. 217 oversized guestrooms, two dining rooms; a lounge and twenty-four-hour-a-day room service.

DIRECTIONS: Take I-95 north toward Wilmington and get off at exit 7, marked Route 52, Delaware Avenue. From right-hand lane take exit 7 onto Adams Street. At the third traffic light turn right onto Eleventh Street, follow Eleventh Street in the middle lane through six traffic lights; Hotel du Pont is on the right. Valet parking is available at the hotel's entrance. For self-parking, turn left onto Orange Street; car park is on the left.

The Inn at Montchanin Village

Not far from the ritzy Hotel du Pont is another historical inn with a du Pont connection, the Inn at Montchanin. Formerly a housing complex for Du Pont employees in the early part of the twentieth century, the attractively restored cottages and the main inn have been converted into a rustic country estate.

The rustic charm of the Inn at Montchanin in the bucolic Brandywine River Valley. *Steve Foxwell*

Located on the scenic byway Route 100, which is dotted with country inns, taverns, and antique shops, and roughly a fifteen-minute drive from the Hotel du Pont, the inn, listed on the National Register of Historic Places is the namesake of Alexandrine de Montchanin, grandmother of the founder of the DuPont Gunpowder Company.

By 1859 the village had two tenant houses, a blacksmith shop where Krazy Kat's

Route 100 and Kirk Road
Montchanin, DE 19710
Tel: 1-800-269-2473,
(302)-888-2133
www.montchanin.com
$$$$
142 miles/2½ hours

is now located, and a workshop. Eleven restored buildings now make up the village-like complex where an old rail depot and Krazy Kat's Restaurant, one of the Brandywine's most original dining spots, are located. Clever portraits of cats adorn the whimsical restaurant that draws crowds from Philadelphia and Washington on weekends. Reservations are strongly recommended for those travelers not registered at the inn.

The inn offers twenty-seven guest rooms and suites with each room designed and decorated differently with period antiques; some of the rooms offer cathedral ceilings. The stone fireplace in the lobby area is an inviting spot for afternoon tea or morning coffee. The inn is a member of both the National Trust's Historic Hotels group and Small Luxury Hotels of the World.

Exposed brick walls, stone fireplaces, four-poster beds, gas fireplaces in some of the guest rooms, and a genuine country ambience make the Montchanin an ideal stopover for travelers. Five miles north of Wilmington, the inn is halfway between New York and Washington with Philadelphia an easy thirty-minute drive. It is conveniently near all of the major sights and attractions including Longwood Gardens, the Brandywine River Museum, and Winterthur.

The Inn at Montchanin Village

ACCOMMODATIONS: Elegant country inn. Twenty-seven guest rooms and suites. Dining room.

DIRECTIONS: Take I-95 north to exit 7 for Delaware Avenue and Route 52 north. At the fourth light turn left on Route 52 (Pennsylvania Avenue); stay in the left lanes at the fork and continue 2.2 miles. Turn right on Route 100 north and continue for 1.5 miles. The inn will be on your right.

Excursions & Diversions

The Wyeth and Du Pont legacies live on in the Brandywine River Valley, where a host of museums and cultural gems prove inviting for visitors desiring a country ambience mixed with first-rate culture. Art enthusiasts and avid gardeners will appreciate the Brandywine River Museum, Longwood Gardens, and Winterthur, three nearby cultural venues that are worth lengthy visits.

Pierre S. du Pont, inspired by the great gardens of Europe, created Longwood Gardens, a living work of art and tribute to nature. A horticultural masterpiece with its winding garden pathways, flower-filled conservatory, and ornate fountains, it is the East Coast's premier garden conservatory.

The glass-enclosed conservatory is Longwood's centerpiece where abundant blooming flowers of the various seasons adorn its interior. At Christmastime brilliant poinsettias and elaborately decorated Christmas trees create a holiday wonderland. Twinkling Christmas lights surrounded by a profusion of tulips, narcissus, and cyclamens accentuate the gleaming Crystal Palace. Christmas trees festooned with Victorian decorations and 400,000 tiny lights outside the conservatory add to the holiday atmosphere.

Sixty full-time gardeners maintain the lushness and immaculate floral beauty of Longwood, including its Orchid Room and pastel-colored lily ponds, which are spectacular in the spring. The six-hundred-foot-long Flower Garden Walk that flanks the country estate was one of du Pont's initial efforts at Longwood, proving ideal for an afternoon stroll.

Nearby are Winterthur—the estate of Henry Francis du Pont, with its outstanding collection of Early American decorative arts—and the Brandywine

River Museum in Chadds Ford, Pennsylvania, famed for its paintings by three generations of Wyeths—N. C., Andrew, and Jamie.

The pastoral and rolling Brandywine River Valley—named after the wine-colored waterway that weaves throughout its landscape—has been the inspiration for countless paintings, drawings, and watercolors by America's most celebrated artistic dynasty, the Wyeths.

The museum, opened in 1971 in a nineteenth-century former gristmill, artfully showcases the work of the Wyeths as well as other important American artists.

Tucked away off Route 1, the scenic byway that weaves through the sculpted landscape past an assortment of antique shops and inns, the museum overlooks the banks of the Brandywine River. The museum is devoted almost entirely to the Wyeths, though its collection also includes more than 2,500 works by other noted artists including Maxfield Parrish, Charles Dana Gibson of Gibson Girl fame, and Frederick Remington, renowned for his classic cowboy bronzes.

The museum is also a showcase of its parent organization, the Brandywine Conservancy, a public-spirited organization founded in 1967 to protect open space and the area's water resources. Wildflower gardens and plants native to the Brandywine surround the museum.

Inside, paintings, watercolors, and illustrations representing the heritage of the Brandywine Valley area are a large part of the museum's growing collection. Among them are nineteenth-century landscapes by William Trost Richards and still lifes by George Cope and Michael Harnett.

The museum, which attracts more than 200,000 visitors annually, handsomely showcases the range and diversity of the Wyeths' talent. Here are N. C. Wyeth's meticulous illustrations of Robert Louis Stevenson's novels, Andrew Wyeth's haunting paintings of nearby Kuerners Farm, and Jamie Wyeth's wistful *Iris at Sea* and his pensive portrait of John F. Kennedy. Three floors of galleries exhibiting original beams and wide floorboards accent artworks inside. A cozy café overlooking the river serves light refreshments and snacks, and the bookstore houses one of the most impressive collections of art-related books in the Brandywine.

From late spring through early October one can also visit N. C. Wyeth's studio, a short tram ride from the museum. Here is where the artist completed most of his important works, including the illustrations for Scribner's collection of Robert Louis Stevenson's works. A guided tour through the studio enables the visitor to get a clearer insight into the range of N. C. Wyeth's talents as both a painter and an illustrator. The studio, restored to the way it looked in 1945, tells the story of the artist and his immense creative legacy. Artist's props, canvases, and old paintbrushes used by the master can be observed on a visit.

Wilmington's thriving riverfront is another venue worth exploring following a day at the museums. Plans are under way to house the Wilmington Art Museum in a section of the First USA Riverfront Arts Center.

The restoration of the riverfront area is one of Wilmington's latest projects. A walk along the Riverwalk—a 1.3-mile waterfront path—affords access to the attractions along the Christina River. Along the preserved pathway one can explore Tubman-Garrett Riverfront Park and the Shipyard Shops.

The First USA Riverfront Arts Center stages a variety of first-rate exhibitions throughout the year. Previous shows exhibited the talents of Russian artisan and jeweler Peter Carl Fabergé and collections borrowed from the Paris Maritime Museum. Plans are for the Wilmington Art Museum to house its collection in one section of the complex.

Also along the waterway one can see the *Kalmar-Nyckel,* a Swedish tall ship moored at the pier, and the Delaware Center for Contemporary Arts, where several galleries featuring twenty-six artists in residence can be discovered. The Delaware Theatre Company is also in the neighborhood.

The Greater Wilmington Convention and Visitors Bureau

100 West Tenth Street
Suite 20
Wilmington, DE 19801
Tel: (302) 652-4088, 1-800-489-6664
www.wilmcvb.org

CHAPTER 3 *Maryland*

ANNAPOLIS
Historic Inns of Annapolis

Imagine a wave of bright and brilliant billowing sails gliding across the Chesapeake Bay and you have one stunning snapshot of Maryland's rich seaport heritage. The sea and the Chesapeake Bay, the largest estuary in the United States, are forever intertwined in the scenic seaport villages of Annapolis, Oxford, and St. Michaels. All three of these utterly appealing nautical towns steeped in seafaring history are exceptional weekend outings. Annapolis is a favorite haunt for Washingtonians. Easy to reach, scenic, and filled with activities, the seaport is a natural for a weekend getaway. Year-round sailing events make the capital city a nonstop destination for sailing enthusiasts. In May a profusion of flower baskets adorns shops and doorways ushering in the spring season, and during the Yuletide season the annual Eastport Yacht Club Sailboats Lights Parade sails by on the Severn.

The Chesapeake Bay inspired lobby of the Maryland Inn in Annapolis.
Historic Inns of Annapolis

58 State Circle
Annapolis, MD 21401
Tel: (410) 263-2641,
1-800-847-8882
www.historicinnsofannapolis
.com
$$$
45 miles/1 hour

Fishermen and yachtsmen alike gravitate to these waterfront destinations that expertly capture Marylanders' love of the sea. Annapolis, by far the most famous, displays vintage taverns, the U.S. Naval Academy, yachts by the hundreds in the summertime, and the Historic Inns of Annapolis.

Known as the "sailing capital of America," Annapolis is teeming with bountiful seafood restaurants; restored Colonial architecture along its narrow, winding streets; and storied naval history within its boundaries.

Founded in 1649 by a group of Puritans from Virginia, Anne Arundel became the wealthy capital of Maryland in 1695. Adopting the name Annapolis in honor of Princess Anne, daughter of King James II, the seaport city flourished from the outset, bringing maritime trade and commerce into the harbor town.

Historic Inns of Annapolis is at the center of the historic district where the State House, St. John's College, the U.S. Naval Academy, historical homes, and a bronze, life-size statue of Alex Haley, who set the beginning of his Pulitzer Prize–winning book, *Roots*, in Annapolis, can be savored and enjoyed. In fact, Haley's enthralling tale of his ancestor, Kunta Kinte, is only one aspect of Annapolis's rich African American heritage.

The Banneker-Douglass Museum of African American History studies and showcases the life and many contributions of Annapolis's and Marylanders' African American citizens. A monument to the United States' first African American Supreme Court justice, Thurgood Marshall, is located on Lawyers Row near the State House. And the town is the only Colonial site where the homes of all the state's signers of the Declaration of Independence—Thomas Stone, William Paca, Samuel Chase, and Charles Carroll—can be found.

But no discussion of Annapolis is complete without highlighting the U.S. Naval Academy, the cornerstone and architectural centerpiece of Annapolis. Founded in 1845 as a school for naval officers and designated a National Historic Landmark, the U.S. Naval Academy, with its broad sweeping lawns, time-honored traditions, and magnificent architecture, defines the very soul of Annapolis.

The campus, or the "Yard," as the midshipmen call it, features a bust of Tecumseh, Bancroft Hall, and the U.S. Naval Academy Chapel, designed by New York architect Ernest Flagg and built in 1904. A monumental structure with its domed roof and large anchors flanking its imposing bronze doorway, the chapel, often referred to as the "Cathedral of the Navy," is the clear standout on a stroll through the Yard.

The real treasures and glory of the chapel are found within its interior where expansive and immaculately restored Tiffany stained-glass windows and a high altar, along with the crypt of John Paul Jones, Revolutionary war hero and father of the modern Navy, can be seen.

The Armel-Leftwich Visitors Center inside Gate 1 is the recommended route for beginning your Naval Academy expedition. A film, gift shop, and organized walking tours of the academy are all found at this location. Also within the Yard is Preble Hall, site of the U.S. Naval Academy Museum, which expertly highlights the Navy and its role in the twentieth century. Within walking distance of here are the Historic Inns of Annapolis, a sure bet for getting a genuine flavor of Annapolis's history and heritage.

Long the favorite for visiting yachtsmen, state legislators, and history buffs, three buildings, the Governor Calvert, Maryland Inn, and Robert Johnson House, make up the engaging structure, which has become a mainstay on the architectural walking tours. The Inn is composed of three buildings, all featuring eighteenth century architecture. The Maryland Inn was originally built as a residence in 1765 and has been transformed many times. Two of its inns face the Maryland State House, where the Treaty of Paris was signed in 1784. The inns' oldest section is the Governor Calvert House, constructed in 1727.

The inns' history is as illuminating and appealing as the 124 guest rooms and suites, which are all designed with a distinctive Colonial flair and period antiques. Eleven delegates of the 1786 Congress stayed at the Maryland Inn, and the Governor Calvert House was once the residence of two former Maryland governors. The Treaty of Paris Restaurant with its lanterns, fireplace, hunting scenes, and low ceilings, is one of Annapolis's favorite dining spots, and the King of France Tavern is an ideal locale for jazz and music enthusiasts.

In May 1973, the Maryland Inn opened the King of France Tavern with guitarist Charlie Byrd and his trio. In fact, music has been the backbone of the tavern's resounding success, as a string of well-known performers including Earl "Fatha" Hines, Ella Fitzgerald, and the Ink Spots has put the cozy enclave on the music map. Things get so heated up on Saturday nights that lines form outside the door early in the evening for hearing jazz greats and musical legends. The inn's proximity to the State House has made it an ongoing favorite with the Maryland Legislature as well, and it is often reported that as many laws are written in the Treaty of Paris Restaurant as in the State House itself.

In addition to their prime central location within the historic district, the inns' other appealing factors include a shuttle van that will scoot guests to local sites. Complimentary tea and coffee are offered to guests opting for concierge-level service.

Historic Inns of Annapolis

ACCOMMODATIONS: Maryland Inn—44 rooms; Governor Calvert House—51 guest rooms; Robert Johnson House—25 guest rooms. Restaurants and lounge.

DIRECTIONS: Annapolis is less than an hour from the Capital Beltway. Take US 50 east toward Annapolis to Rowe Blvd. south, exit 24, toward Annapolis and merge onto Maryland 70 east. Turn left onto College Ave. Turn right on North Street and merge into State Circle. The Maryland Inn will be on your right, three quarters of the way around the circle.

Excursions & Diversions

While exploring Annapolis on foot is highly desirable and enjoyable, getting out on the bay is a real treat for landlubbers wanting to get a taste of all that the Chesapeake has to offer. Day sailings are available with Schooner Woodwind Cruises and Watermark Cruises the most popular. The Schooner Woodwind Cruises depart from the Annapolis Marriott for two-hour sails on the Chesapeake Bay. They also offer day sails to St. Michaels during the spring, summer, and fall seasons. The two-masted schooner sails around the Chesapeake Bay offering a selection of breakfast cruises and an assortment of day sailings.

Watermark Cruises offers forty- and ninety-minute narrated boat tours around the Annapolis Harbor, Severn River, Spa Creek, the banks of the U.S. Naval Academy and on to the historic Thomas Point Lighthouse. Watermark also offers seven-and-a-half-hour "Day on the Bay" cruises to St. Michaels or Baltimore's Inner Harbor.

The "Day on the Bay" is one of its most popular outings, encompassing a trip to St. Michaels and the Eastern Shore where visitors have time to explore the Maritime Museum and the shops of St. Michaels. Various vessels are enlisted for these tours, but any trip on the bay is pure pleasure for sailing and boating fans.

Annapolis and Anne Arundel County Conference and Visitors Bureau

26 West Street
Annapolis, MD 21401
Tel: (410) 280-0445
www.visit-annapolis.org
www.schoonerwoodwind.com
www.watermarkcruises.com

BALTIMORE

Radisson Plaza Lord Baltimore Hotel

Maryland's glistening port city has experienced an ongoing renaissance since the early 1970s, when massive funding spearheaded by then mayor Donald William Schaefer revitalized the Inner Harbor.

Once dominated by decaying wharfs and empty storefronts, the Rouse Developments' creation of Harborplace, a bustling shopping and dining complex, set Baltimore's facelift in motion. Following the success of Harborplace, the Baltimore National Aquarium sealed the deal for Baltimore, making it a magnet for tourists.

A surge in renovating and restoring areas surrounding the waterfront continues today where a host of ambitious projects are on the drawing board through 2004. The momentum embraced by Baltimoreans has been the driving force behind the city's unparalleled success as a favorite getaway destination for Washingtonians.

Slightly more than a one-hour drive from Washington via the Baltimore-Washington Parkway and I-95, Baltimore has finally come into its own as a thriving metropolitan area. Where previously fleets of sailing

The towering brick structure of Baltimore's most historic hotel is within easy reach of the Inner Harbor. *Trish Foxwell*

20 West Baltimore Street
Baltimore, MD 21201
Tel: (410) 539-8400
1-800-333-3333 (Radisson)
$$$$
50 miles/1¼ hour
www.radisson.com

ships and schooners dominated Baltimore's commerce, today tourism is at the helm of its unstoppable success. No longer overshadowed by the nation's capital as a tourist draw, the Inner Harbor, its centerpiece, is filled with a string of new hotels, the Power Plant shopping complex, and two envied sports arenas, Camden Yards and Ravens Stadium, all the more reason to visit Maryland's largest and most dynamic destination.

Within walking distance of the busy Inner Harbor is the Radisson Plaza Lord Baltimore, Baltimore's oldest hotel. Opened in 1928 by hotel owner Harry Busick, the Radisson is another prime example of Baltimoreans' determination to preserve valuable architectural buildings while construction of new sites continues in and around the Inner Harbor.

The Radisson embodies architectural elements reminiscent of early-twentieth-century hotels. It was the sole remaining high-rise building to be built with classical architecture. Listed on the National Register in 1982, the hotel was sold in 1960 to the New York–based Weissberg chain. In 1984 Saul Perlmutter purchased the hotel and eventually sold it to its present owner, the Radisson Hotel chain.

Like many city hotels of its generation, the Radisson has undergone a series of setbacks. It was largely due to the Inner Harbor's success that the hotel regained its stature as a favorite meeting place for Baltimoreans and city officials who have used the hotel as campaign headquarters.

The Radisson, along with the Belvedere Hotel, the city's other 1920s architectural landmark (now a condo), is one of the city's most important buildings recalling Baltimore's Art Deco period. Reminders of the hotel's Art Deco period remain visible today; a large crystal Art Deco chandelier is found at the hotel's lobby entrance.

The twenty-three–story structure with its 439 guest rooms has been completely remodeled with pastel colors, chintz fabrics, and design touches borrowed from the Art Deco period. While the hotel has maintained the beauty of its bygone days, it has successfully implemented all of the modern amenities one expects from a AAA Four-Diamond hotel. A concierge level includes both continental breakfast and afternoon tea, with the Lord Baltimore Grill serving up the best weekday lunch buffet in the city.

While many of the hotel's records have been lost during several ownerships, it is believed that the imposing brick structure was a favorite haunt of Baltimore's social elite and the literary set during the 1920s and '30s. The many famous literary names associated with the hotel include novelist F. Scott Fitzgerald, humorist and *Baltimore Sun* columnist H. L. Mencken, and Dashiell Hammett, author of the *Maltese Falcon,* who worked as a Pinkerton detective in Baltimore prior to his literary fame.

Other documented facts regarding the hotel's rich history include civil rights leader Martin Luther King's delivery of an impassioned speech in the hotel's ballroom during the 1960s and the use of the hotel as campaign head-quarters for various governors of Maryland.

Radisson Plaza Lord Baltimore

ACCOMMODATIONS: 424 guest rooms, concierge valet parking, fitness center and sauna. Restaurants and room service.

DIRECTIONS: The hotel is located in downtown Baltimore, three blocks from the Inner Harbor, about one hour's driving time from Washington. Take I-95 north to Baltimore/New York. As you approach Baltimore, merge onto I-395 north at exit 53 toward downtown. This turns into South Howard Street. Turn right onto West Baltimore Street.

Admiral Fell Inn

Just beyond the clamor and commotion of the Inner Harbor is Fells Point. A "village within a village" best describes Baltimore's most recognized and colorful waterfront community.

A maritime setting awaits visitors to the intimate Admiral Fell Inn in Baltimore's historic waterfront district. *Steve Foxwell*

Once the neighborhood of Frederick Douglass and singer Billie Holliday, Fells Point brings into sharp focus Baltimore's importance as a thriving shipbuilding port in the 1800s. At one time no fewer than thirteen shipyards occupied the waterfront, including the one responsible for constructing the supersleek *Baltimore Clipper.*

Many of the ships built at Fells Point played a significant role in both the Revolutionary War and the War of 1812. In one of his diaries John Adams wrote, "Today I walked out to Fells Point, the place where all of the ships lay."

888 South Broadway
Baltimore, MD 21231
Tel: 1-800-292-4667,
(410) 522-7377
www.admiralfell.com
$$$
50 miles/1¼ hours

With the profusion of sailing vessels and schooners came officers, seamen, and travelers, and with them came the need for housing. The tiny Admiral Fell Inn, named after William Fell, an English land speculator who purchased the land in 1726 and who did not hold the title of admiral, is composed of eight adjoining brick buildings, some dating back to the 1700s. Originally known as the Anchorage and later the Seamen's YMCA, the Federalist townhouse-style inn offers eighty rooms, some featuring whirlpools, where the décor is predominantly Chippendale and Queen Anne furniture.

The attractive and utterly appealing inn, with its deep-forest-green lobby accented with maritime paintings, celebrates Baltimore's maritime past unlike any other lodging spot in the city. A lobby fireplace, tea and coffee available throughout the day, a European-style breakfast, and the acclaimed Hamilton's Restaurant specializing in Maryland seafood delicacies are among the inn's amenities. For guests who want to step back in time, the Admiral Fell Inn is the best bet in Baltimore. Belgian blocks, brick sidewalks, antique shops, and art galleries outline its exterior where once bawdy bars and boardinghouses stood. Although the fact is not recorded, it is believed that while living in the city poet Edgar Allan Poe, who lived on Amity Street, was a regular visitor.

Opened in 1985 and completely refurbished and renovated in 1996, the inn is recognized as a National Historic Landmark. Adjoining the inn is the equally appealing Petticoat Tea Room. Separately owned and operated from the hotel, the tearoom serves casual fare from tea sandwiches to a wide variety of teas. From here one can easily scoot over on the water taxi to the Inner Harbor in minutes, avoiding city traffic. At dusk Fells Point becomes a hub for nightlife when the city's office workers and residents frequent the many cafés and taverns found here.

The Admiral Fell Inn

ACCOMMODATIONS: An urban inn with eighty guest rooms and suites. Continental breakfast, courtesy van service to the Inner Harbor and other downtown locations. Dining room and tearoom.

DIRECTIONS: From I-95 north off the beltway, take exit 53 and follow the signs for Inner Harbor/Downtown. After you pass Oriole Park at Camden Yards, turn right onto Pratt Street. Follow Pratt to President Street and turn right. Follow President to Eastern Ave and turn right. The inn is four blocks ahead on the right.

Peabody Court Hotel

Baltimore's profusion of small boutique hotels is impressive, with the Peabody Court its newest addition. A Clarion Collection Hotel and member of the National Trust's Historic Hotel group, the Peabody Court with its handsome Renaissance Revival facade recently completed a $3 million restoration. Old World charm and grace personify its appeal.

The hotel is a testament to the glamorous style associated with the 1920s, and a six-foot Baccarat chandelier and George Peabody's paneled library greet one at its entrance. The Peabody Court was originally the home of Robert Garrett, one of the principal organizers of the B&O Railroad, the first railroad in the nation. Garrett willed the home to his daughter Mary, who endowed it to the Johns Hopkins Hospital with the condition that the university admit women to its medical school. The building was demolished in the 1920s; the present building was built in 1928.

The 104-guest-room hotel was originally a luxury apartment house in 1928 for the fashionable Mt. Vernon neighborhood.

Historic Mt. Vernon Square is one of the sights near the Peabody Court Hotel. *Steve Foxwell*

612 Cathedral Street
Baltimore, MD 21201
1-800-292-5500
Tel: (410) 727-7101
$$$$
51 miles/1¼ hours
www.peabodycourt
.snbhotels.com

Named after Massachusetts-born Baltimorean philanthropist George Peabody, the Peabody Court's preferred location at Mt. Vernon Place offers a nice diversion from the crowds found at the bustling Inner Harbor hotels and for those travelers desiring understated luxury in a beautiful locale.

This is the neighborhood where novelist F. Scott Fitzgerald would often take walks while living in the city.

Centrally located, the Peabody Court includes an opulent presidential suite and five queen suites. All of the rooms feature original French veneer marble-topped furniture and lavish marble bathrooms, while the public areas display refurbished original artwork, marble, and tile work reminiscent of the 1920s.

The hotel's stylish restaurant, George's on Mt. Vernon Square, recaptures the drawing room atmosphere and is another reason to visit. Named after the three Georges of Baltimore, George Washington, George Peabody, and George "Babe Ruth" Herman, the restaurant specializes in American cuisine.

The hotel's rooftop Washington Club, formerly the Citronelle Restaurant, is available for special events. Sweeping views of Baltimore through its floor-to-ceiling windows add to its appeal as a private meeting venue.

The Peabody Court

ACCOMMODATIONS: One of the Clarion Hotel chain, this elegant boutique hotel offers 104 newly renovated guest rooms and a popular restaurant open for breakfast, lunch, and dinner.

DIRECTIONS: From I-95 north, take the Pratt Street exit. Turn left onto Charles Street, then left onto West Mt. Vernon Place. Proceed to Cathedral Street and turn left.

Excursions & Diversions

For literary enthusiasts or for those travelers seeking to escape the crowds at the Inner Harbor, Baltimore serves up a rich repository for exploring the city's many literary haunts. Following in Fitzgerald's, Mencken's, and Poe's footsteps is an easy outing from the Radisson Plaza Lord Baltimore Hotel, the Peabody Court Hotel, or the Admiral Fell Inn.

Beginning with Fitzgerald, who arrived in Baltimore in 1932 and lived in the city until 1934, Baltimore has abundant sites related to the Jazz Age novelist. Baltimore became a welcome refuge to the novelist, who came to the city for a variety of personal reasons. Fitzgerald, who described himself as "the last of the novelists," resided at 1307 Park Avenue in the fashionable Bolton Hill neighborhood with his daughter, Scottie, while his wife, Zelda, was being treated at Phipps Clinic.

The home, a private residence, is where Fitzgerald put the finishing touches on *Tender Is the Night*. While Fitzgerald was living in the town house, Max Perkins, John Dos Passos, John O'Hara, and Gertrude Stein visited him.

Some other Fitzgerald landmarks in and around town include the Owl Bar at the Belvedere, a hotel during Fitzgerald's lifetime and presently a condo. The Owl Bar is where the writer met with Baltimore native, friend, and mentor H. L. Mencken, swapping stories and having a drink or two while engaging in conversation. Fitzgerald's and Mencken's wives, Zelda Sayre and Sara Haardt, were both from Montgomery, Alabama, and close friends.

The Francis Scott Key Monument at Eutaw Place is another key Fitzgerald site. A distant relative of Key on his father's side, Fitzgerald often went for long walks around the towering monument. Fitzgerald, along with his wife, Zelda, and daughter, Scottie, is buried at St. Mary's Cemetery in Rockville, Maryland, where the last two lines from *The Great Gatsby* are inscribed on his tombstone.

The H. L. Mencken sites are sprinkled throughout Baltimore and include the Owl Bar at the Belvedere and, more importantly, Mencken's lifetime residence at 1524 Hollins Street. The Bard of Baltimore's life can be explored on a visit. For seventy of his seventy-five years, Mencken lived in the nineteenth-century row house with his brother August except for a brief tenure when he lived with his wife, Sara Haardt, on Cathedral Street. Placques throughout the row house display examples of Mencken's acerbic wit. The writer's daily ritual consisted of a cold bath, breakfast, work, and a beer or two with the boys at 10 P.M. The home has limited visiting hours.

Mencken did most of his writing both for the *Baltimore Sun* and his various books in his second-floor study. Correspondence to friends Ezra Pound, Theodore Dreiser, and Upton Sinclair was composed in the book-lined study. The Mencken Room at the Enoch Pratt Library contains the most extensive collection of Mencken's works, letters, and documents in the country.

In 1948 Mencken, who described his newspaper career as the "maddest, gladdest, damndest existence ever enjoyed by mortal youth," suffered a stroke from which he never fully recovered. He died in 1956, and his ashes are buried at the Loudoun Park Cemetery in Baltimore.

Baltimore's most celebrated literary figure, Edgar Allan Poe, is associated with several sites. Poe was born in Boston and raised in Richmond. His Baltimore years, 1832 to 1835, were some of his most satisfying and productive. The house at 203 Amity Street is where Poe completed eleven tales and the poem "The Raven," which is believed to have been composed in the garret of the tiny abode. Poe came to live with his aunt, Maria Clemm, at the house. It was during his tenure here that he explored a variety of literary genres and mastered his poetry.

Poe's gravesite can be found at the Westminster Church Cemetery. Every year on the eve of Poe's birthday, January 19, a cloaked and mysterious phantom leaves a glass of cognac and a rose atop Poe's tombstone. The American poet, ranked as one of the nation's greatest literary voices, left Baltimore in 1835 only to return in 1849, the year of his mysterious death. The events surrounding Poe's death are debated to this day. Found semiconscious in a doorway near Camden Yard, Poe was transported to Washington General Hospital, where he died on October 7, 1849. He is buried beside his wife Virginia Clemm and his aunt, Maria Clemm.

The Baltimore Convention and Visitors Bureau

100 Light Street
12th Floor
Baltimore, MD 21202
Tel: 1-877-BALTIMORE
www.baltimore.org

OXFORD
The Robert Morris Inn

Like its sister community, St. Michaels, sixteen miles away, Oxford is a sailing town where quaint country lanes, rolling farmland, and an old-fashioned flavor make the tranquil community a haven for artists, writers, and travelers seeking relief from the madding crowds of Ocean City.

Nestled in Talbot County and overlooking the Tred Avon River, Oxford is a microcosm of America's past. Settled by English merchants from London, Liverpool, and Bristol, Oxford was second only to Annapolis as a port city in the 1700s.

The inn is named after Robert Morris, financier of the American Revolution and signer of the Declaration of Independence, who was also the benefactor of the Liverpool Trading House. Morris built his Oxford home with his fortune; part of the original residence has been incorporated into the inn.

In the inn, which is a tribute to the beauty of eighteenth-century architecture, hand-hewn beams and remnants of its illustrious past can be enjoyed.

Author James Michener became a regular to Oxford's enchanting Robert Morris Inn. *George Gardner*

P.O. Box 70
314 N. Morris St.
Oxford, MD 21654
Tel: (410) 226-5111
   1-888-823-4012
www.robertmorrisinn.com
$$$
120 miles/2 hours

Throughout its history the inn has been used as a private residence, town hall, boardinghouse, and general store. By the late 1940s the inn began to function as a country inn, paving the way for the Robert Morris Inn.

Today the inn is owned and operated by Wendy and Ken Dixon, who have been its owners and innkeepers for thirty years.

The setting alone is part of the inn's enduring appeal, which so charmed author James Michener that he settled in the area while writing *Chesapeake*.

The inn has fourteen rooms with four of the rooms offering side views of the Tred Avon River. These are the 1710 rooms and display original paneling with the larger rooms offering king-size beds and adjoining sitting rooms. The largest Colonial corner room comes with slanted doorways, a fireplace made from bricks of a ship's ballast, and original paneling. A four-poster canopy bed with a side view of the river makes this the best room in the house. The Colonial décor is prevalent throughout all of the rooms where period antiques and artifacts make travelers feel that they are revisiting the eighteenth century.

The hauntingly beautiful landscape of the Eastern Shore is the backdrop for Michener's novel *Chesapeake*. His love affair with the Eastern Shore stemmed from his college days when he sailed the Chesapeake Bay. It was at the Robert Morris Inn's tavern that Michener wrote the original outline for *Chesapeake*. But it was the inn's famous crab cakes that lured him back time and time again to the tavern. He claimed that they were the best he had ever tasted, according to the Gibsons, who became lifelong friends with the writer. They mailed him crab cakes while he was in Alaska writing *Alaska*.

In addition to the Michener story many other interesting tales are associated with this Eastern Shore landmark. While a senator, Barry Goldwater often drove over from Washington for the crab cakes, and in the 1970s Susan Ford, daughter of former president Gerald Ford, traveled to Oxford aboard a boat with the Secret Service. Frogmen had to check for bombs underneath the ferry dock and set up a command post in one of the guest bedrooms. Crooner Bing Crosby

---

The Robert Morris Inn

ACCOMMODATIONS: Fourteen historic rooms in the main inn, plus nineteen in the Sandaway Lodge and other buildings one-half block from the main inn. Many with water views. No phones or TVs in the rooms. Dining room.

DIRECTIONS: Take the Beltway (I-495) to Route 50 toward Annapolis. Cross the Bay Bridge and continue on Route 50 east to Easton. About twenty-six miles from the bridge, bear right on Route 322. Go 3.3 miles. Turn right on Route 333 south. Oxford is 8.5 miles, and the inn is at the end of the road on your right just before the ferry dock. If you arrive by boat from the Chesapeake Bay, enter the Choptank River and follow on the Tred Avon River.

---

also enjoyed a visit while in town to film *American Sportsman* with Kurt Gowdy. Crosby and Gowdy ate a crab cake lunch before heading back to filming.

Excursions & Diversions

Renting a kayak or opting for a ferry ride are a couple of great options while in residence at the Robert Morris Inn. During the summer months sailing charters can be arranged through the inn as well as a variety of other outdoor activities. One can easily reach St. Michaels by the Oxford-Bellevue Ferry, the oldest privately run ferry in the nation.

The Eastern Shore has abundant things to see and do all year long, from the very popular Waterfowl Festival held in neighboring Easton during the fall migration to the Tilghman Island Christmas parade where a flotilla of lighted boats passes through the harbor. Tilghman Island is also a hot spot for monarch butterflies, which stop here every August on their migration to Mexico. Oxford stages its own lighted boat parade in early December where St. Nicholas signals the start of the holiday season. Sparkling lights and decorated boats make this event an annual favorite.

Talbot County Chamber of Commerce

P.O. Box 1366
Easton Plaza Suite 53
Easton, MD 21601
Tel: (410) 822-4653
www.talbotchamber.org

SHARPSBURG
The Inn at Antietam

Fields of valor surround the Inn at Antietam where in the springtime azaleas frame the white-columned hideaway that sits on the fringes of the historic battlefield.

An ideal retreat for Civil War enthusiasts, the 1908 Eastlake Victorian inn boasts five individually designed suites, all with bedroom, sitting room, and private bath. Furnishings in the Victorian manner define the tranquility found at the inn, which is a member of the Maryland Bed and Breakfast Association and the Civil War Preservation Trust.

The stillness of the Antietam Battlefield accents a visit to the Inn at Antietam. *Paul G. Beswick*

P.O. Box 119
220 East Main St.
Sharpsburg, MD 21782
Tel: (301) 432-6601
1-877-835-6011
www.innatantietam.com
$$$
70 miles/1½ hours

Owned and operated by innkeepers Bob LeBlanc and Charles Van Metre, the Inn at Antietam combines the best of both worlds, a luxurious woodsy setting coupled with the profound history of Antietam.

The inn, which opened in 1984, offers a flower-laden veranda and sumptuous parlor revealing Victorian charm. In the parlor a glass of sherry is offered nightly to guests with a roaring fire in the background. Closed for the month of January, at Christmastime the inn is adorned in holiday splendor, complete with garlands of Victorian Christmas decorations and a towering Christmas tree.

The Rose Suite and the General Burnside Smokehouse Suite are the most beautiful accommodations. The General Burnside Smokehouse Suite displays large overstuffed chairs in front of a brick fireplace. The Rose Suite is festively decorated with a floral décor and four-poster bed.

Breakfast specialties include Belgian waffles and blueberry pancakes made from scratch, served with the genuine hospitality of the inn's gracious and accommodating innkeepers.

The Inn at Antietam

DIRECTIONS: From Washington take I-270 north to I-70 junction at Frederick. From Frederick follow I-70 west to exit 35 (Route 66), turn left onto Route 66 and go six miles to Boonsboro. At the second traffic light turn right onto Route 34 and continue six miles to Sharpsburg. You will see the Antietam National Cemetery on the left. The Inn at Antietam is located just past the Antietam National Cemetery.

Excursions & Diversions

Visiting the hallowed hills of the Antietam National Battlefield, which in 2003 commemorates its 141st anniversary, opens a window into one of the Civil War's most pivotal and important battles. The battle on September 17, 1862 between 41,000 Confederate and 87,000 Union troops is considered the bloodiest single-day battle in American history. The battle turned the tide of the war in favor of the Union forces and enabled Lincoln to announce the abolition of slavery in the South. It is considered by many historians to have led to the beginning of the end for the Confederates.

The battlefield, minutes from the Inn at Antietam and a twenty-five-minute drive south of Hagerstown, Maryland, on Route 65, was the site of Gen. Robert E. Lee's first invasion of the North following his victory eighteen days earlier at the Second Battle of Manassas.

The visitors center houses a museum, an observation room, a 134-seat theater, a bookstore, and a research library. The center, which is open every day except Thanksgiving, Christmas, and New Year's Day from 8:30 A.M. to 5 P.M. September to May and until 6. P.M. June through August, is an ideal place to begin your Civil War journey.

An all-inclusive park entrance fee of $3 per adult or $5 per family (children under 16 free) is required. The excellent *Antietam Visit* film is shown every thirty minutes except at noon and 12:30, when the *Antietam Documentary* is presented. *Antietam Visit* is a twenty-six-minute movie re-creating the battle as well as President Abraham Lincoln's visit to the Union commander Gen. George B. McClellan.

The best way to tour the battlefield is to take a self-guided driving tour along the eight-and-a-half mile route with eleven stops detailing the battle. An audiotape can be rented at the visitors center. Markers, tablets, and monuments placed along the driving route offer visitors a comprehensive look at the battle and its key players. The artillery locations mark where the five hundred cannons used in the battle were located.

Washington County Convention and Visitors Bureau

Elizabeth Hager Center
16 Public Square
Hagerstown, MD 21740
Tel: (301) 791-3246, 1-888-257-2600
www.marylandmemories.org

ST. MICHAELS
The Inn at Perry Cabin

Across the towering Chesapeake Bay Bridge connecting Annapolis to Maryland's Eastern Shore is the picturesque sailing village of St. Michaels.

The namesake of an English parish, St. Michaels is a paradise for yachters and for those travelers seeking to savor life at a more leisurely and relaxed pace. Largely serving as a trading post for trappers and farmers in its early days, St. Michaels' finest and most heroic moment was during the War of 1812 when its determined residents kept British barges from firing cannon shot into the town by cleverly hoisting lanterns into ships' masts and into the trees behind the town tricking their enemy into overshooting the town, and saving the scenic seaport from destruction.

Named after Commodore Perry, the Inn at Perry Cabin is a favorite for sailors with its dock entrance. *Orient Express Hotels*

308 Watkins Lane
St. Michaels, MD 21663
Tel: (410) 745-2200;
1-800-722-2949
www.innatperrycabin.com
$$$$
81 miles/2 hours

Incorporated as a town in 1607, St. Michaels hosts a flotilla of sailboats during the summer months, when crowds often gather near the Maritime Museum to enjoy a day in one of Maryland's geographic treasures. Narrow streets lined with Victorian and Colonial houses along Talbot Street, its main thoroughfare, take one back to a time when skipjacks and Baltimore clippers ruled the seas.

Once a thriving shipbuilding port, today the town boasts antique shops, Christ Episcopal Church, the Chesapeake Maritime Museum, and the Hooper Strait Lighthouse. Within minutes of Talbot Street is the Inn at Perry Cabin, part of the Orient Express Hotel Group, and St. Michaels' loveliest and most luxurious place to drop anchor for the night.

Built following the War of 1812, the inn, appropriately named after Commodore Perry, whose loyal purser and aide-de-camp, Samuel Hambleton, built the inn's north wing to resemble Perry's cabin on the flagship USS *Niagara*, has catered to diplomats, dignitaries, and Hollywood stars. Former prime minister

Margaret Thatcher, along with actors Joanne Woodward and Paul Newman, have visited and enjoyed the pastoral waterfront setting on numerous visits.

The inn's graceful white Colonial Revival architecture evokes a bygone era when sailors and yachtsmen wandered the tiny streets of St. Michaels following a day at sea. Overlooking the serene Miles River, a tributary of the Chesapeake Bay, the inn is situated on twenty-five waterfront acres. Its inviting rooms with fine period antiques, some offering canopy beds, fireplaces, and cathedral ceilings, make a visit similar to staying in a very well appointed ancestral estate.

A recent $15 million expansion and facelift completed in 2002 increased the inn's total guestrooms to eighty. The private dock area is of particular appeal to yachtsmen, who can slip their vessels up to 110 feet long into the convenient slips. An indoor swimming pool, library, and croquet lawn accentuate the relaxing nature of the property.

A range of activities awaits visitors to the inn, including fishing charters, sailing excursions, horse-drawn carriage rides, and golfing at nearby courses. Considered a luxury boutique property, the inn, named one of the top twelve inns by *Country Inns Magazine*, combines the beauty of the Chesapeake with elegantly designed rooms all displaying a nautical theme.

The Ashley Room serves breakfast, lunch, and dinner daily, while the Miles Room offers a dining alternative, including alfresco dining, weather permitting. The chef and his culinary team are also prepared to pack a gourmet picnic basket to take on sailing excursions or hops around St. Michaels. The "Bounty of the Bay" basket is a favorite, containing the inn's signature crab spring roll paired with smoked bluefish and crusty bread; the "Saturday in the Park" basket is a favorite for families. Fried chicken, potato salad, and coleslaw are included in this treat.

The Inn at Perry Cabin

DIRECTIONS: From the Capital Beltway take Route 50 east across the Chesapeake Bay Bridge. Stay on Route 50 at the Route 50/301 split; go approximately thirty miles to the town of Easton. One-half mile beyond the Easton Airport bear right to Route 322; go two miles. At traffic light turn right onto Route 33 to St. Michaels; go through St. Michaels, and the inn is located on the right. Driving time is just under two hours.

Excursions & Diversions

A nautical theme prevails throughout the Eastern Shore. The Chesapeake Bay Maritime Museum, which houses the world's largest collection of traditional bay boats, brings to life the Chesapeake Bay. A lighthouse, working boatyard, and hands-on displays reveal the role the bay has played in history from the golden age of steamboats to today's sailing vessels. Another unique feature is the Lighthouse Overnights offered by the museum whereby groups can arrange to stay in the Hooper Strait Lighthouse, which is part of the museum, on Friday or Saturday nights in April, May, September, and October. A maximum of fifteen people can stay in the lighthouse, which must be booked one year in advance.

A sailing tour on the Chesapeake Bay aboard the *H. M. Krentz,* an authentic working skipjack, is a step back in time to when skipjacks dredged the Chesapeake for oysters. Skipjacks are the last working boats operated under sail in the United States.

The Chesapeake Bay Maritime Museum, Inc.

Mill Street
P.O. Box 636
St. Michaels, MD 21663
Tel: (410) 745-2916
www.cbmm.org

Chesapeake Skipjack Sailing Charters H. M. Krentz

Captain Ed Farley
P.O. Box 582
St. Michaels, MD 21663
Tel: (410) 745-6080
www.oystercatcher.com

Talbot County Chamber of Commerce

P.O. Box 1366
Easton Plaza Suite 53
Easton, MD 21601
Tel: (410) 822-4653
www.talbotchamber.org

TANEYTOWN
Antrim 1844 Inn

Taneytown, a stone's throw from Gettysburg, Pennsylvania, is home to Antrim 1844 Inn, once a private residence and now one of Carroll County's loveliest and most desirable inns.

Originally a plantation built in 1844 by Col. Andrew Ege, the property changed hands on the eve of the Civil War in 1861 when George Washington Clabaugh, chief justice of the Supreme Court, purchased the house. Nestled in the Catoctin Mountains, Gen. George Meade of the Union army watched from one of the inn's windows as his army marched to the Battle of Gettysburg.

Owned by the Clabaugh/Lamberton family until 1961, the inn, registered as a National Historic Landmark, along with the several outbuildings surrounding the main mansion, has been restored by owners Dorothy and Richard Mollett, who have successfully recaptured the ambience of antebellum hospitality in a quiet, forested setting. The Greek Revival–style mansion exhibits Federal influences throughout its interior where period antiques accent the guest rooms.

The bucolic Maryland countryside surrounds the Antrim 1844.
Antrim 1844

30 Trevanian Road
Taneytown, MD 21787
Tel: 1-800-858-1844;
(410) 756-6812
www.antrim1844.com
$$$
120 miles/2 hours

Within the main inn, or mansion, are nine rooms reserved for guests where antique beds, fireplaces, and panoramic views of the central Maryland countryside make for an unforgettable visit. The surrounding outbuildings prove every bit as appealing as the main inn for accommodations; the buildings offer thirteen additional guest rooms, each with its own fireplace.

The Ice House near the formal gardens has an English cottage atmosphere, whereas the Smith House offers two suites with fireplaces, balconies, and an executive suite in the English basement. The Carriage House proves the most enchanting place to stay over the weekend. The most recent restoration project on the premises, the Carriage House offers suites with names associated with Civil War leaders.

The U. S. Grant Suite and the Robert E. Lee Suite are the largest at the inn, with the Lee Suite offering courtyard views and a spacious sitting room. The Reynolds Room is one of the loveliest suites in the Carriage House, with expansive Palladian windows overlooking a forested area. The Sleigh Room is the prettiest of all, where a wood-burning fireplace and private deck overlooking a stream afford one absolute privacy. Surrounded by twenty-three acres, Antrim 1844 also offers a host of activities including croquet, tennis, horseshoes, and swimming in its outdoor pool.

The room rate includes a full breakfast where hearty Belgian waffles might be on the menu. During the fall and winter seasons dinner is served in the Smokehouse, where brick floors and large fireplaces add to the inn's rustic atmosphere. A six-course dinner prepared by the inn's chef is served nightly to guests. The inn's Pickford Pub serves drinks and cigars in a cozy setting.

Antrim 1844 Inn

ACCOMMODATIONS: Bed-and-breakfast. Nine restored rooms in the mansion; thirteen in surrounding unique outbuildings. Each room has a fireplace and private bath. Children over twelve are welcome.

DIRECTIONS: From Washington take I-495 to I-270 west toward Frederick. Take Route 15 north toward Gettysburg. Go to Route 140 east toward Taneytown. In Taneytown go through the stoplight and over the railroad tracks. In 1/8 mile the road splits; bear right on Trevanion road and proceed 150 feet to the first set of brick pillars. Turn right and follow the signs for parking.

Excursions & Diversions

Twelve miles south of the inn is Gettysburg, a premier Civil War stop and location of the Dwight D. Eisenhower Historic Site.

Plan on spending an entire day touring these enthralling attractions, which showcase important elements associated with both Civil War and

World War II history. An auto tour through the major points of the battlefield is available from the Gettysburg National Park Center Visitors Center. More than 1,300 markers and monuments dot the hallowed battlefield, which was the site of a pivotal battle during the Civil War. The fifty-foot-high mural painted in 1884 depicting Pickett's Charge is not to be missed in the Gettysburg Cyclorama across from the visitors center.

A convenient shuttle bus transports visitors to the former home of President Dwight Eisenhower. A brief biographical film detailing the life and accomplishments of the former president can be enjoyed on a tour through the house and gardens. The sprawling residence, purchased by Eisenhower in 1950, is a 189-acre farm on the fringes of the Gettysburg battlefield.

The house served as a presidential retreat, temporary White House, and meeting place for world leaders including Sir Winston Churchill. All of the items and furnishings in the house belonged to the former president. The porch, Eisenhower's favorite room for meeting foreign dignitaries and world leaders, is a highlight on a tour. Ranger tours encompassing a variety of subjects detail the former president's life from his illustrious military career to his presidency, the Cold War, and hobbies.

At Christmastime the home is decorated in the Eisenhower tradition from December 1–31. The self-guided walks around the grounds prove every bit as interesting as the house tour. Numbered stops include the PGA putting green, rose gardens, guesthouse, and a garage, which still houses Eisenhower's Jeep, golf carts, and station wagon.

Gettysburg Convention and Visitors Bureau

35 Carlisle Street
Gettysburg, PA 17325
Tel: (717) 334-6274
www.gettysburg.com

Eisenhower Home Information:

www.nps.gov/eise/home.htm

CHAPTER 4 *Washington, D.C.*

WASHINGTON, DC

Renowned for its rich collection of monuments and museums, the Federal City is also endowed with a wealth of historic hotels. The city, largely mapped out by French architect Pierre Charles L'Enfant in 1791 at the request of George Washington, is a visually stunning city displaying abundant panoramic views and sites detailing American history.

Although L'Enfant was eventually relieved of his duties several years following his commission as the city's premier architect and designer, his brilliant blueprints for a symmetrical design were executed in 1889 where ultimately his plan of the U.S. Capitol overlooking the Mall became a reality for effectively showcasing Washington's sweeping vistas. The sprawling Mall area with the Smithsonian Institutions, National Gallery of Art, and U.S. Capitol in the near distance defines the center of political and cultural Washington.

A colorful tapestry of eclectic neighborhoods from Georgetown's "cave dwellers" to the ethnic diversity of Adams Morgan to Embassy Row with its diplomatic embassies and consulates comprises some of Washington's more interesting areas. Four very distinctive landmark hotels all within a few blocks of one another recall the city's storied past. The Hay-Adams, Henley Park, Jefferson, Mayflower, Morrison-Clark Inn, Phoenix Park, St. Regis, and Willard Inter-Continental are treasured architectural landmarks in Washington. It is not by chance that these eight hotels within close reach of the White House reveal enthralling chapters in the city's history.

The Hay-Adams

The Hay-Adams, reopened in March 2002 after a multimillion-dollar facelift, and the St. Regis (formerly the Carlton Hotel) are directly across the street from one another on Sixteenth Street. Both hotels incorporated the handiwork of Washington developer Harry Wardman and Turkish architect Mihran Mesrobian. The Hay-Adams with its bird's-eye views of the White House and many of its rooms overlooking Lafayette Square has been a mainstay of importance in Washington.

Named after John Hay, President Abraham Lincoln's private secretary, and Henry Adams, great-grandson of John Adams, the hotel now stands on the site of the homes of the two men.

Following Hay's death in 1905, Senator James Wadsworth purchased the property. Upon Adams's death in 1918, his house became the Brazilian embassy.

In 1927 all that changed when Washington developer and real-estate tycoon Henry Wardman tore down both proper-

A handsome brass lantern greets guests to the Hay Adams.
Trish Foxwell

One Lafayette Square
Sixteenth and H Streets, N.W,
Washington, DC 20006
Tel: (202) 638-6600 or
1-800-853-6807
www.hayadams.com
$$$$$

ties to construct the Hay-Adams House. The 200-room Italian Renaissance apartment hotel, designed by Mirhan Mesrobian, cost $90,000 to build. Opened to the public in 1928, the hotel, with its marble baths, kitchens, and many amenities, attracted the likes of Charles Lindbergh, Amelia Earhart, Ethel Barrymore, and Sinclair Lewis in its early years. Many well-known newscasters, including Peter Jennings, Tom Brokaw, and Dan Rather, frequently use the top-floor suites for getting White House views during important broadcasts.

Refurbished and renovated at a cost of $18 million in March 2002 and reopened following a four-month closing, the Hay-Adams now offers two secure floors for visiting dignitaries and other high-profile guests. Each of the 145 guest rooms has also been spruced up. Fine tapestries, ornamental fireplaces, and balconies in selected rooms make a visit similar to staying in someone's private town house with all of the amenities one expects of a modern hotel. The Hay-Adams dining room, the Lafayette Room, has also been revamped and remodeled and offers American/ Continental cuisine. A AAA Four-Diamond Hotel and recipient of *Condé Nast Traveler*'s Gold List of best places to stay, the Hay-Adams is owned and operated by Hospitality Visions, LLC.

A variety of packages are offered throughout the year, with many highlighting the sights of Washington, special events, or themed weekends.

The Hay-Adams Hotel

ACCOMMODATIONS: Elegant city hotel. 145 rooms and suites; valet parking, concierge, health club privileges. Restaurant and wine bar.

LOCATION: On Lafayette Square across from the White House, within walking distance of sightseeing, shopping, and Metrorail.

The Henley Park Hotel

The sister hotel of the Morrison-Clark Inn, the Henley Park is another Massachusetts Avenue landmark. Its unique Tudor-style architecture featuring 118 gargoyles makes it a standout in Washington's downtown area.

Leaded-glass windows, a Mercer tile floor, and intricate and elaborate moldings accent its English-boarding-school appearance. Inside one will find all of the amenities associated with a four-star hotel.

The Eton Room, a banquet facility, personifies its pronounced English influences.

Originally known as the Tudor Hall Apartments, catering to discerning senators and congressmen who used the handsome facility as their home away from home, the building became a hotel in 1982. Its richly appointed guest rooms are distinctively decorated with an English country house motif complete with furniture reproductions of Hepplewhite, Chippendale, and Queen Anne furnishings.

The entrance to the Henley Park Hotel. *The Henley Park Hotel*

926 Massachusetts Ave., N.W.
Washington, DC 20001
Tel: Reservations—
1-800-222-8474;
(202) 638-5200
www.henleypark.com
$$$$

The Henley Park, namesake of England's Henley-on-the-Thames, is reminiscent of Brown's Hotel in London. Its guest rooms are designed in English country style, displaying rich chintzes, period antiques, and Old World charm.

The hotel's European exterior is by far its most captivating element. A family of gargoyles (believed to ward off evil spirits), greets guests at its Massachusetts Avenue entrance. Four transplanted gargoyles, now located above the Coeur de Lion Restaurant, were rescued from New York's Commodore Hotel. A brilliant skylight atrium adorned by chandeliers and natural-brick-faced walls make the restaurant one of the hotel's most appealing features.

The Coeur de Lion, opened in 1983, presents innovative California cuisine in an intimate setting. Well known for attracting power brokers and

Washington's elite, on any given night a famous face might be spotted in the crowd.

The Blue Bar, the inn's chic jazz nightspot, features a live jazz trio on weekends, while the hotel's more refined Wilkes Room exhibits a drawing-room atmosphere.

The Henley Park Hotel

ACCOMMODATIONS: Boutique hotel with 96 guestrooms; valet parking, complimentary downtown sedan service (weekdays). Restaurant and lounge.

LOCATION: Downtown Washington near the MCI Center. Convenient to sightseeing and museums.

The Jefferson Hotel

Perhaps one of Washington's best-kept secrets is the discreet and discriminating luxury found at the Jefferson.

Quiet elegance aptly describes the hundred-room boutique hotel, which was originally constructed as an apartment house catering to discerning diplomats and dignitaries.

The Jefferson's pedigreed bloodline can be traced back to 1922 when the understated Beaux Arts building was designed by Jules Henri de Sibour, a direct descendant of France's King Louis XVI.

Completed the following year at a cost of $450,000, the hotel provides a welcome refuge and retreat for travelers desiring privacy amidst luxurious surroundings.

In the center of Washington's Embassy Row neighborhood is the graceful arched doorway of the Jefferson Hotel. *The Jefferson Hotel*

Far removed from the hustle and bustle of Sixteenth Street, the hotel was purchased by Gen. A. B. Glancy in 1931. Glancy eventually turned the property into military housing during World War II.

The Jefferson's heyday was in 1955 when it opened its doors to the public, quickly at-

**1200 Sixteenth Street, N.W.
Washington, DC 20036
Tel: (202) 347-2200
1-866-308-1200
www.loewshotel.com
$$$$**

tracting Hollywood stars and Washington dignitaries alike who viewed the hotel as a safe haven from the ambitious Washington press corps members who frequently camped outside its doors to see who was in town.

By the 1970s Edward Bennett Williams, attorney and former owner of the Baltimore Orioles, bought the hotel, which had for many years been his social meeting place. Williams's plans for the Jefferson were modeled after London's famed Connaught Hotel, which he considered to offer the best of everything in hotel accommodations.

Investing $7 million in renovations, Williams added priceless antiques, art, and artifacts to the Jefferson, making its appearance similar to a fine Washington townhouse instead of a hotel.

Williams wanted the Jefferson to be the finest that Washington had to offer and added his own personal tastes and touches to the hotel's interior, making it the preferred residence for anyone who was anyone in the city.

Under his proprietorship and watchful eye, all rooms were individually decorated, and original Thomas Jefferson documents along with a crystal chandelier that once hung in the Willard Hotel were added to the hotel's repository of treasures. A personal ambience prevailed during the Williams era, making the Jefferson the choice for best-selling authors, Hollywood celebrities, and visiting statesmen, who felt at home in the elegant and comfortable surroundings.

Presently owned by Loew's Hotels, the Jefferson has a history that features a long list of luminaries ranging from Washington's power elite to acclaimed musicians.

During Ronald Reagan's presidency the Jefferson earned the title of "White House north" because of the many high-ranking government officials and cabinet members who made the hotel their Washington residence when in town. During the Iran-contra trials, Oliver North secretly stayed at the Jefferson to avoid the reporters who were following his every move. When George H. W. Bush was inaugurated, almost every member of the Bush clan stayed at the hotel. Former secretary of the treasury Robert Rubin used the hotel as his Washington base during the 1980s, and talk show host Larry King broadcast many of his radio shows from the Jefferson.

One evening not too long ago musician Billy Joel, in town for a concert, tickled the ivories on the Jefferson's lounge piano with few in attendance. The hotel continues to house long-term guests, whom it calls "Jeffersonians," who keep the Mobil Four-Star and AAA Four-Diamond property on its toes.

Its location close to the National Geographic Society and the Russian embassy and four blocks from the White House makes the hotel handy for sightseeing.

The hundred guest rooms, including thirty suites, display the same attention to detail that Williams initially envisioned. Marble bathrooms, plush terry bathrobes, twice-daily maid service, and a bilingiual staff make the Jefferson a perpetual favorite.

The sixty-seat dining room displays eighteenth-century historical prints and portraits, many of which previously hung in the White House and Blair House, while the lounge offers afternoon tea and late-night cordials. Guests can use the fitness facilities of the membership-based University Club, which is conveniently located across the street from the hotel.

The Jefferson Hotel

ACCOMMODATIONS: A Loews' Hotel. One hundred guestrooms and suites; twenty-four-hour concierge, health facilities. Restaurant.

LOCATION: Downtown Washington, four blocks from the White House.

The Mayflower Hotel

Charles Lindbergh's whirlwind cross-country tour following his historic Atlantic crossing took him to Washington and the Mayflower Hotel on June 13, 1927.

Everywhere the young fresh-faced aviator appeared, adulation soon followed, and the nation's capital proved no different. Feted by President Calvin Coolidge and treated like the conquering hero, the shy and retiring Lindbergh attended a breakfast at the Mayflower given in his honor by the National Aeronautic Association.

The breakfast, served at 7 a.m. sharp, paid tribute to the pilot who had captured the hearts and imagination of the American public. People lined up outside the Mayflower's Connecticut Avenue entrance hoping to catch a glimpse of the country's newest and brightest hero.

The Grand Ballroom was brimming with members of the press, diplomats, dignitaries, and members of Congress when the lanky Minnesotan sauntered in to claim his hero's welcome.

The sweeping promenade of the Mayflower Hotel's lobby. *The Mayflower Hotel*

A Marriott Renaissance Hotel
1127 Connecticut Ave., N.W.
Washington, DC 20036
Tel: (202) 347-3000;
  1-800-228-9290/7697
www.renaissancehotels.com
$$$$$

Lindbergh, presented with the National Geographic Society's Hubbard Medal, breezed among the throngs of admiring guests both inside and outside the ballroom. While "Lucky Lindy's" visit is certainly one of the Mayflower's major historical highlights, it is not by far the only tale worth telling. and his name is joined by an impressive list of other important names.

The Mayflower, opened two years prior to Lindbergh's visit by Washington hotelier and entrepreneur Allan E. Walker, was built with one mission in mind: to be the most elegant meeting place for the world's most important guests. The visionary developer and real-estate baron felt that the Connecticut Avenue location was ideally suited for discerning guests, diplomats, and dignitaries. Being only four blocks from the White House added to its alluring appeal and stature.

Following its grand opening in 1925, the Mayflower, with its long promenade and pronounced European touches, became the "belle of the ball" for many inaugural balls, beginning with President Calvin Coolidge's charity inaugural ball on March 4, 1925. The Mayflower's first official event, catering to some six thousand guests, became the hotel's signature event for years to come, giving it the unofficial title of "the Inaugural Ball Hotel." Coolidge's absence due to the death of his young son, John, did not detract from the star-studded society event that had all of Washington talking.

Another banner year in the hotel's history came several years later in 1932 when Democrat and President-elect Franklin Delano Roosevelt, along with his wife, Eleanor, and family, camped out at the hotel prior to his inauguration. Suite 776 became known as the Roosevelt Suite; here the future president penned his inaugural address. Roosevelt's ongoing affection for the Mayflower began during his term as governor of New York when the aspiring politician chose the hotel to conduct his Washington business.

Many Roosevelt-related events took place at the Mayflower during Roosevelt's presidency. Following the Japanese attack on Pearl Harbor in 1941, the hotel became the glamorous backdrop for many social gatherings including various fund-raising events geared to the war effort. Hollywood stars Marlene Dietrich, Van Johnson, and George Murphy presented numerous benefit shows at the Mayflower during World War II, and song-and-dance man Gene Kelly also got involved when he threw a lavish war-bond benefit in 1942. In 1944 a grand birthday bash was held for Roosevelt with Eleanor cutting the cake. Mickey Rooney, Tyrone Power, Olivia De Haviland, and other popular stars of the day participated in the highly publicized event.

In short, the Mayflower earned a reputation as the "Democrats' hotel" because so many well-known Democrats in addition to Roosevelt held events at the hotel. Other important Democrats soon followed in FDR's footsteps to the Mayflower. Harry Truman announced his bid for the presidency at the Jackson Day dinner in 1948, and prior to JFK's 1961 inauguration, Jack and Jackie Kennedy were feted at a party hosted by the president-elect's father, Joseph P. Kennedy. The Kennedy story continues on Inauguration Day 1961 when a blizzard blanketed the city, leaving many guests stranded at the Mayflower following the inaugural ball. The hotel was filled to capacity, and many hallways, corridors, and nooks and crannies became a camping-out ground for guests.

FBI Director J. Edgar Hoover had lunch at the Mayflower every day for twenty years while he was at the helm of the bureau. Movie actress Jean Harlow spent a morning at the hotel's switchboard as an operator during her visit, and Winston Churchill sat for his portrait at the Mayflower. Aviatrix Amelia Earhart chose the hotel when she received the special Gold Medal of the National Geographic Society for her solo flight across the Atlantic.

From 1946 to 1956 the Mayflower was owned and operated by Hilton Hotel Corp. The once grande dame of Washington lost much of its luster during this period, and the promenade became a tired rendition of 1950s decor. In 1966 things turned around for the property when it was purchased by May Wash Associates, which began the task of restoring the time-worn structure. In a major restoration effort begun in 1981, architects consulted original floor plans, historic descriptions, and old photographs to restore the Mayflower to its architectural beauty.

Domed skylights were reopened, murals were revealed and restored, and two seventeenth-century Aubusson tapestries were returned to the promenade. With the major restoration in place by 1984 the Mayflower, a Mobil Four-Star, AAA Four-Diamond hotel now owned by Marriott Renaissance Hotels, began a new chapter in its history. Listed on the National Register of Historic Places, in 1993 the hotel underwent another multimillion-dollar refurbishment of the 330-room west wing. On the mezzanine level is a small museum of photographs and mementos detailing the Mayflower's history and some of its noted guests.

The Mayflower Hotel

ACCOMMODATIONS: Elegant city hotel with 660 guest rooms including 78 junior suites, 2 grand suites (the Presidential Suite and the Mayflower Suite). Dining at Cafe Promenade, Town and Country Lounge, Lobby Court.

LOCATION: Downtown Washington convenient to dining, shopping, and sightseeing. Near Metrorail.

Morrison-Clark Inn

Reminding one of Washington's Victorian era, the Morrison-Clark Historic Inn holds the coveted title of being the only inn in the city to be listed on the National Register of Historic Places.

Dating back to the Civil War period, the inn is composed of two separate historic houses totaling forty-one guest rooms and thirteen suites.

Situated one block from the new convention center, which opened in the spring of 2003, the hotel is named after two Washington businessmen, David Morrison and Reuben Clark, who bought the posh townhouses in 1864.

The inn, opened in 1983, is owned and operated by Classic Hospitality. It encompasses vintage segments of Washington's history beginning in 1923 when the Women's Army and Navy League purchased the home, converting it into an inexpensive lodging place for America's enlisted men. Initially the home accommodated 120 servicemen at the bargain rate of 75 cents a night. In 1954 the property became known as the Soldiers, Sailors, Marines, and Airmen's Club.

The intimate elegance of a bedroom suite at the Morrison Clark Inn in downtown Washington.
The Morrison Clark Inn

1015 L Street, N.W.
Washington, DC 20001
Reservations: 1-800-332-7898;
(202) 898-1200
www.morrisonclark.com
$$$$

Traditionally, first ladies presided over the club where teas and fundraisers helped to defray the club's operating costs. Every first lady from Mrs. Calvin Coolidge to Mrs. Ronald Reagan served as the club's honorary chairperson.

A French country motif with pine armoires, wicker furnishings, and quilts can be found in the guest rooms. The Deluxe Rooms feature Neoclassical designs with desks and armoires highlighted by muted taupe fabrics.

The seventy-five-seat Victorian Dining Room with its carved marble fireplaces, ten-foot gilded mirrors, and lace curtains has been selected as one of Washington's finest by *Gourmet* magazine; the restaurant specializes in American cuisine. The inn's Club Room is an ideal place for cocktails.

Morrison-Clark Inn

ACCOMMODATIONS: Elegant urban inn with 54 guest rooms and suites. Fitness center, valet parking, restaurant.

LOCATION: At Eleventh and L Streets in downtown Washington, convenient to local attractions.

The Phoenix Park Hotel

A touch of Ireland can be savored at the utterly charming Phoenix Park Hotel, which sits on Capitol Hill's doorstep across from Union Station.

Named after a 1,760-acre park in Dublin beside the River Liffey, the hotel offers 149 guest rooms reflecting the aura of an exceptionally fine eighteenth-century Irish country estate. Gleaming woods, original oil paintings, marble staircases, and Irish linens and crystal can be found in both the private and public areas.

The front entrance to the Irish-inspired Phoenix Park Hotel with the U.S. Capitol Dome in the background. *The Phoenix Park Hotel*

520 North Capitol Street, N.W.
Washington, DC 20001
Reservations: 1-800-824-5419
Tel: (202) 638-6900
$$$$
www.phoenixparkhotel.com

Resembling a little corner of Ireland in the heart of Washington, the hotel has been the site of meetings of power brokers, congressmen, and senators since 1922.

Its proximity to Capitol Hill (some suites offer breathtaking views of the Capitol dome) has attracted a wealth of politicians throughout its reign as the Hill's most charming accommodation. Former president Bill Clinton, Senator Edward Kennedy, Vice President Dick Cheney, Newt Gingrich, Senator John Kerry, and Senator Joe Lieberman are but a few of the politicians to have visited or dined at the property.

Former Speaker of the House of Representatives Tip O'Neill celebrated his eightieth birthday party at the hotel, which has also seen Senator Hillary Rodham Clinton, who dropped in while first lady. Diplomats have also used the hotel as their Washington lodging spot; among them is the Irish deputy minister Dick Spring, who uses the Capitol Hill address on his visits to Washington.

The property was launched as the Phoenix Park Hotel in 1982 under the stewardship of Irish American entrepreneur Dan Coleman. A second wing was added to the original building in 1997.

General Manager Joseph Zarza is usually the first one to greet guests to the hotel. His warm hospitality has become legendary amongst politicians who use the hotel for a variety of fund-raisers, social events, and parties.

Gaelic influences are found everywhere in the upscale European boutique hotel. The three penthouse suites feature balconies overlooking Union Station, working fireplaces, and richly burnished mahogany antiques. Each of the two-story suites features a parlor and a winding spiral staircase that ascends to a deluxe king bedroom with a full bath.

A very popular gathering place, particularly on St. Patrick's Day, is the Dubliner pub, the hotel's hot dining spot, which is a favorite for Capitol Hill staffers with its stunning bar imported from Dublin and an assortment of Irish ales.

Ranked as the city's premier genuine Irish pub, the Dubliner, established in 1974, is the country's leading purveyor of Guinness Stout and the sole purveyor of Auld Dubliner Amber Ale, imported exclusively from Dublin. But having a "cup of cheer" is only one treat in store on a visit. Fish and chips along with freshly made Irish stew make the Dubliner a choice dining spot as well.

At night the Dubliner becomes a stage for a variety of Irish entertainers, and beloved Irish folk songs accompany an evening meal.

In warmer months café tables line the pub's patio, reminding guests of an authentic Dublin city pub.

With all its Irish elegance and superb service (many of the hotel's staff hail from Ireland), a friendly and inviting atmosphere makes the Phoenix Park and the Dubliner a favorite with Washingtonians. Unlike some of the city's posh hotels, the Phoenix Park offers all of the amenities of a four-star hotel without the attitude.

The phrase "When Irish eyes are smiling" can be applied to its able and accommodating staff, who will go out of their way to make sure you return again and again.

The Phoenix Park Hotel

ACCOMMODATIONS: 149 guest rooms and suites; fitness center, concierge, room service. Restaurant and lounge.

LOCATION: Near Capitol Hill, one block from Union Station (Amtrak and Metrorail).

The St. Regis

The St. Regis, modeled after Claridge's in London, is two blocks from the White House. President Calvin Coolidge cut the ceremonial ribbon opening the hotel on October 1, 1926.

The hotel was designated a National Historical Place in 1991, and more than $25 million was spent in 1995 to update and renovate the hotel's 193 rooms and suites. The hotel's ornate lobby, resplendent with Louis XV chandeliers and intricately carved gilded ceilings, reminds one of the diplomatic reception rooms found in the palaces of Europe. European touches are found everywhere throughout, from its Italian Renaissance exterior to the garden courtyard reminiscent of Florence and Venice.

The handsomely appointed lobby of the St. Regis Hotel. *Trish Foxwell*

923 Sixteenth & K Streets, N.W.
Washington, DC 20006
Tel: (202) 638-2626
1-800-325-3535
www.sheraton.com
$$$$$

Opened at the height of the Jazz Age, the St. Regis was the center of social Washington in its heyday during the 1930s and '40s. Every U.S. president since Coolidge has visited or held state functions at the St. Regis, a regular haunt of Washington's "Old Guard" establishment. But during the Great Depression, the hotel, like much of Washington and the rest of the nation, fell on hard times, and Henry Wardman, who had made a fortune in Washington's booming real estate market prior to the economic downturn, was no exception. Wardman lost the St. Regis in 1932, and labor leader John L. Lewis, who set up his union headquarters at the hotel, kept the luxurious landmark in business.

Both the Roosevelt and Truman administrations enjoyed significant ties to the hotel. Roosevelt's secretary of state, Cordell Hull, and his wife lived and entertained at the St. Regis. During their residency the lobby was usually bustling with curious onlookers, all wanting to catch a glimpse of a cabinet member. When the White House underwent a renovation during Truman's era, the St. Regis became the glamorous backdrop for a host of parties and state dinners. Visitors never knew who they would run into when the Hulls were in town.

General John J. "Black Jack" Pershing, the World War I hero, also had ties to the St. Regis. He spent Thanksgiving 1942 at the hotel while a patient at Walter Reed Army Hospital. Pershing, who frequented the hotel, was not about to endure hospital food on the Thanksgiving holiday. Plans were made to accommodate the general, and throngs of admirers applauded him as he entered the dining room. Pershing preferred the hotel to all others in Washington and stayed there following his White House visits with the president.

Royalty and Hollywood also came calling at the elegant hostelry. When Britain's Queen Elizabeth II visited the St. Regis during George H. W. Bush's administration, the hotel became the setting for the queen's private reception. The Duke and Duchess of Windsor, Princess Grace of Monaco, and Prince Edward and his wife, Sophie, also made the St. Regis their Washington address while visiting the city.

Singer Dinah Shore made the hotel's dining room her preferred venue for meeting members of the press. And actress Joan Crawford, while married to the CEO of Pepsi Corp., insisted that only Pepsi products be used in the St. Regis while she was in residence. John F. Kennedy Jr. and his wife, Carolyn Bessette Kennedy, stayed at the hotel during their many Washington visits. During Bill Clinton's 1993 inauguration, the Rock the Vote Ball was held at the hotel with actors Richard Gere, Tom Cruise, and Kim Basinger in attendance.

The Crystal Ballroom, with its lavishly embellished, hand-stenciled ceiling and sparkling crystal chandeliers overlooking the Italian Renaissance Garden, continues to be a favorite gathering place for social and diplomatic Washington. While business slacked off considerably following the September 11, 2001, tragedy because of its proximity to the White House, the St. Regis is once again attracting discriminating travelers.

The St. Regis

ACCOMMODATIONS: A Starwood Hotel (part of the Sheraton Hotel group). Elegant city hotel with 143 rooms and suites, twenty-four-hour room service, fitness center, restaurant.

LOCATION: Corner of Sixteenth and K Streets, convenient to attractions, dining and shopping.

The Willard InterContinental Hotel

Few hotels in Washington can match the storied history of the Willard. Two blocks from the White House, the hotel was boarded up during the 1960s and would have fallen to the wrecking ball had it not been for the Oliver Carr Co., which miraculously saved the stately structure.

Restored to its former glory, the Willard reopened on August 20, 1986, after more than twenty years of being boarded up. The Willard has been a magnet for power brokers and diplomats along with a long list of literary names throughout its history.

Named after Henry Willard, who purchased the property in 1850, the hotel as we know it today was constructed in 1901 and remains at the center of social and political Washington. The hotel's main claim to fame is not only its striking and magnificent Beaux Arts architecture designed by Henry Janeway Hardenbergh, who also designed New York's Plaza Hotel and the Waldorf-Astoria, but also the fact that since 1853 it has hosted every U.S. president from Franklin Pierce to Bill Clinton.

The Willard InterContinental Hotel: Afternoon sun accents the gleaming marble lobby of the Willard Inter-Continental Hotel. *Trish Foxwell*

1401 Pennsylvania Ave., N.W.
Washington, DC 20004
Tel: (202) 628-9100
   1-800-327-0200
www.washington.inter
   conti.com
$$$$$

Author Nathaniel Hawthorne, who stayed at the hotel while covering the Civil War for the *Atlantic Monthly,* is only one of the illustrious literary figures associated with the Willard. Hawthorne wrote, "This hotel, in fact, may be more justly called the center of Washington and the Union than either the Capitol, the White House, or the State Department.... you exchange nods with governors of sovereign states; you elbow illustrious men, and tread on the toes of generals; you hear statesmen and orators speaking in their familiar tones. You are mixed up with office seekers, wire pullers, inventors, artists, prosers ... until identity is lost among them."

Hawthorne's sentiments remain true today. Important guests from around the globe continue to stay at the Willard, whose proximity to the White House and beautifully appointed guest rooms remain its primary attractions.

One of the Willard's most captivating stories relates to Abraham Lincoln, who prior to his 1861 inauguration was smuggled into the hotel by a Pinkerton detective. Tensions were high around Washington during the Civil War, and it was feared that someone would try to assassinate Lincoln. From February 23, 1861, until Inauguration Day on March 4, Lincoln, along with his family of five, resided at the Willard. Lincoln promptly paid his hotel bill after moving into the White House, no doubt waiting for his first paycheck to arrive.

Another important figure from Lincoln's era was author Julia Ward Howe, who in 1861 was a guest at the hotel. One night Howe was awakened during the night by Union soldiers singing "John Brown's Body" outside her window. Moved by the haunting music, Howe became inspired to write the words for "Battle Hymn of the Republic."

Housing and hosting presidents during the 1860s elevated the Willard to its elite status in Washington. President Ulysses S. Grant is also connected with the hotel. Grant, who frequently sauntered over from the White House to enjoy a cigar and brandy, looked upon the Willard as a respite from the pressures of the presidency. He made the Willard a regular haunt. When word leaked out that the president was spending considerable time at the hotel, everyone from ambitious power brokers to aspiring diplomats and members of the press camped out in the hotel's lobby hoping to get Grant's attention. The term "lobbyist" was coined during Grant's tenure owing to the throngs of policy-makers who wanted to catch the president's ear on various issues.

Among other significant footnotes: President Woodrow Wilson held meetings at the hotel to sculpt his League to Enforce Peace, predecessor of the League of Nations. Calvin Coolidge was so fond of the Willard that he made the hotel his official residence for a month in 1923. Coolidge resided at the Willard while the newly widowed Mrs. Warren Harding, whose husband had been assassinated while in office, packed her belongings to leave the White House.

Presidents are not the only icons of history affiliated with the Willard. Journalists and writers have also spent considerable time at the hotel, most notably in the Round Robin Bar, whose walls are lined with portraits of some of the literary greats who have graced its halls. Mark Twain, Charles Dickens,

Walt Whitman, and Nathaniel Hawthorne delighted in the Willard's many amenities and proximity to the White House and the halls of Congress. Other famous guests include showman P. T. Barnum, Jenny Lind, Flo Ziegfield, Harry Houdini, the Barrymore acting troupe, Mae West, and inventor Samuel Morse.

The Willard InterContinental

ACCOMMODATIONS: Elegant city hotel with 341 guest rooms including 42 suites. Fitness center, business center, restaurants, and lounge.

LOCATION: In the heart of Washington at Fourteenth Street and Pennsylvania Avenue, two blocks from the White House, sight-seeing, dining, and shopping.

Excursions & Diversions

For escaping the madding crowds at the Smithsonian museums, Washington abounds in alternative sight-seeing options. Peering into the lives of some of Washington's more famous residents is made easy by touring both the Hillwood Museum and Gardens and the Woodrow Wilson House in the Embassy Row area of the city.

Hillwood Museum and Gardens, located in northwest Washington off upper Connecticut Avenue, was the home of the late Marjorie Merriweather Post, the Post cereal heiress and Washington socialite.

The impressive thirty-six-room mansion, set on twenty-five acres, which was built in 1926 and purchased by Mrs. Post in 1955, opens a window into one of Washington's more glamorous eras when diplomatic receptions and lavish parties were the order of the day. The brick home is where Post lived until her death in 1973.

A visit affords one the rare opportunity of seeing the largest collection of Russian decorative arts outside Russia. Included in the impressive collection are Russian porcelain, Russian Orthodox icons, silver, portraits, and an assortment of eighty Fabergé items, including two of the famous Fabergé Easter eggs. An audiocassette tour is included in the price of admission, and there is an attractive café on the premises for light snacks and lunch.

A newly expanded visitors center with continuous showings of a film detail-

---

ing Mrs. Post's life and her priceless collection is an ideal introduction to the home and gardens. A trove of Fabergé-like replicas, books about Russia, and copies of Fabergé eggs make a visit to the gift shop a must.

The most enthralling aspect of a visit to Hillwood is seeing Mrs. Post's prized collection, highlighted by state-of-the-art gallery ceiling lighting. A tour through the mansion is similar to walking through someone's private home; personal mementos such as silver-framed photographs add a personal touch to a visit.

Mrs. Post's interest in collecting Russian artifacts began in 1937 when she and her husband, Joseph E. Davies, appointed ambassador to the Soviet Union under President Franklin Roosevelt, moved to Moscow. Post spent hours scouring the attics of Moscow uncovering magnificent items that once belonged to Czar Nicholas II and his family. Upon returning to Washington, she continued her Russian collection and designated that Hillwood, her favorite residence, would become a museum for showcasing her valuable historical artifacts.

The two most interesting rooms are on the main floor: the Russian Porcelain Room and the Icon Room. Row upon row of vividly colored Russian porcelain illuminated in a display case leads one to the Icon Room, certain to be the most visited and outstanding room in the house. In the center of the room stands a display case designed by Fabergé, filled with several of Mrs. Post's most important Fabergé items, including the two Imperial Easter eggs.

The large egg, the pale pink Catherine the Great egg made in 1914, is by far the more striking of the two. Gold, seed pearls, and tiny diamonds encircling the egg make it this room's dazzling centerpiece. Next to it is the Twelve-Monogram Fabergé egg, crafted by Mikhail Perkin, one of Fabergé's chief designers. A brilliant lapis blue enamel egg, it displays twelve diamond-studded monograms of Alexander III and his wife, Maria Fyodorovna. Both were gifts from their son, Nicholas II, Russia's last czar, to his mother. Also in the display case is a statuette of Peter the Great modeled after the one in St. Petersburg. Designed in gold with an emerald base, this is one of Mrs. Post's most valuable acquisitions.

An exploration of other rooms in the house includes the upstairs bedroom, where her evening gowns and Cartier jewelry can be observed along with numerous family photographs of her daughter, Dina, and other family members. The Chinese Garden is another delight for outdoor exploring; here Mrs. Post staged countless dinner parties for her important guests.

Near Hillwood in the vicinity of upper Connecticut Avenue at 2340 S Street, the Woodrow Wilson House, a National Trust site, is the home of the only president to remain in Washington following his White House years.

The house recalls Wilson's life and aspirations and is filled with Wilson memorabilia from his personal library ranging from draft notes outlining the League of Nations to the brass Princeton tiger sculpture that adorns a bookcase in the downstairs study. A grandfather clock chimes hourly on the stairway, and in the upstairs bedroom the familiar fur coat seen so often in photographs of Wilson can be observed.

Framed photographs of historical figures, Wilson's walking cane lying beside his favorite chair, and a lovely breakfast nook overlooking a magnificent garden are some of the highlights on a tour.

People gathered outside the house when Wilson's health began to deteriorate following a stroke. Crowds kept a vigil outside the house until Wilson's death on February 3, 1924.

---

www.woodrowwilsonhouse.org
www.hillwoodmuseum.org
Washington, D.C., Convention and Tourist Corp.
901 7th Street, NW
Suite 600
Washington, DC 20001-3719
Tel: (202) 789-7000
www.washington.org

CHAPTER 5 *Virginia*

CHARLOTTESVILLE

The Boar's Head Inn

The lushly landscaped campus of "Mr. Jefferson's academical village"—the University of Virginia—frames the heart of Charlottesville. A university town in the truest sense, the hilly enclave in the center of Albemarle County is reminiscent of "Old Virginia" at its best. Rambling horse farms, wineries, manor houses, and a pastoral landscape accent the academic atmosphere.

The circular drive entranceway to Charlottesville's most popular country inn. *Trish Foxwell*

**200 Ednam Drive
Charlottesville, VA 22903
Tel: (434) 296-2181,
1-800-476-1988
www.boarsheadinn.com
$$$$
125 miles/2½ hours**

While the visitor is roaming its many winding byways and forested woodlands, the smell of wood-burning fireplaces and lazy autumn afternoons spring to mind. The memory of Thomas Jefferson haunts every corner of the village from Michie Tavern to the Lawn at the University of Virginia and Monticello, Jefferson's proudest architectural achievement.

Two fine lodging choices that capture both the flavor and history of Charlottesville are the Boar's Head Inn, modeled after an English country estate, and Keswick Hall, a grander and statelier property set amidst a sprawling countryside.

The Boar's Head Inn, tucked away on Ednam Drive just minutes from both the university and Monticello, was opened in 1965 by a group of Charlottesville businessmen. Resembling an English country manor house, the somewhat rustic inn displays rough-hewn beamed ceilings and reproduction antiques throughout its public spaces and guest rooms. The AAA Four-Diamond property offering 171 guest rooms sits in the foothills of the Blue Ridge on a 573-acre site surrounded by wineries and antique shops.

The British influences can be seen everywhere throughout the property from the main inn's thirty-nine guest rooms to the Hunt Club's fourteen rooms. The Hunt Club's rooms are the most spacious, offering choice lakeside views from private balconies and terraces. Ednam Hall, a separate building on the premises, has seventy-four guest rooms.

The Old Mill Room, the inn's acclaimed AAA Five-Diamond dining room, displays some of the original fieldstones, pine beams, and planking of the gristmill that once stood on the site. Describing itself as a "country resort at the University of Virginia," the Boar's Head continues to be a popular gathering place for students, faculty, and celebrity residents author John Grisham and actress Sissy Spacek.

The Boar's Head successfully recaptures the spirit and atmosphere of Elizabethan England with all of the amenities one would expect to find at a luxury resort. Golfing at nearby Birdwood Golf Course, hot air ballooning, and a variety of sight-seeing trips can be arranged through the front desk. The fitness center offers twenty indoor and outdoor tennis courts and an outdoor swimming pool open during warmer months. Bike rentals are also available to guests who want to roam the Charlottesville countryside on their own. Children's activities can also be arranged through the front desk.

The Spa is the Boar's Head newest feature. Opened in spring 2003, the 5,000-square-foot facility, designed with an English motif, provides private dressing, steam, and sauna rooms for men and women, a therapy center, and a variety of treatments designed for relaxing in the sublime country setting. The Inn's acclaimed dining room, the Old Mill Room, offers an atmosphere replete with fieldstone, pine beams, and planking.

Some of the former guests linked to the inn include the Dalai Lama, who visited in 1999; Elizabeth Taylor; Sigourney Weaver; and Charlton Heston.

The Boar's Head Inn

ACCOMMODATIONS: 160 rooms, 11 suites, championship golf course, full-service sports club with indoor and outdoor tennis, swimming, state-of-the-art fitness center, and luxury spa.

DIRECTIONS: From DC area take Route 29 south to Charlottesville. Take the Route 250 west bypass to the third exit, Route 250 west. The entrance is one mile on the left.

Located just six miles east of Charlottesville and five miles from Monticello, Keswick Hall offers a completely different experience from the Boar's Head Inn.

While the Boar's Head reminds one of tweedy professors, bookish types, and Parent's Weekend, Keswick Hall is resplendent with Laura Ashley décor, formal tea, and a decidedly more pompous attitude. With its ornate Italianate architecture, the forty-eight-room hotel, set on six hundred acres of Virginia countryside, is part of the Orient Express Hotel Group. It features an eighteen-hole Arnold Palmer signature golf course, an indoor/outdoor pool, fitness center with a spa, and tennis courts. Think *Gosford Park* with Virginia hunt country touches and you have a fairly accurate description of the landed-gentry ambience.

Built as a private residence in 1912 and named Villa Crawford, Keswick Hall was

The country estate exterior of Keswick Hall. *Orient Express Hotels*

701 Club Dr.
Keswick, VA 22947
Tel: (434) 979-3440
www.keswick.com
$$$$$
120 miles/2 hours

converted to a country club in 1930 and closed for ten years. Sir Bernard Ashley, best known as the husband of designer Laura Ashley, bought the property in 1990, tripling its size and adding the golf club. Nine years later the Orient Express Hotel Group signed on and updated the hotel's appearance.

Long hallways, overstuffed furniture, and Laura Ashley's designs dominate Keswick's interior. The Tuscan-style villa on the edge of the Blue Ridge has been a favorite of the Hollywood set, including actor Anthony Hopkins and others desiring privacy in a countryside environment.

The Yellow Morning Room, Drawing Room, and Snooker Room have also been updated. Keswick Hall's guest rooms feature four-poster beds, hand-painted armoires, and period antiques all designed to enhance the flavor of an opulent English estate. Besides the cozy and elegant guest rooms with their sumptuous décor, the golf course, designed in 1939 by Fred Findlay, was completely overhauled and redesigned in 1990 by the Arnold Palmer team.

The Morning Room is a choice nook for a spot of tea or for reading by the fireplace, while the Crawford lounge is the place for meeting fellow guests. Afternoon tea is a ritual here, served in the Drawing Room—a great place to unwind following a day on the links or exploring the Charlottesville countryside. Full-service dining is available at Keswick Hall, with the more understated Palmer Room the choice for light fare.

Keswick Hall

ACCOMMODATIONS: A luxury hotel with forty-eight uniquely decorated guest rooms, two dining rooms, golf course, indoor/outdoor pool, spa, and fitness center.

DIRECTIONS: From Washington take I-66 west, exit at Route 29 Gainesville. Travel on Route 29 south to Charlottesville to Shadwell. At Shadwell make a left turn on Route 22 east. Go 1.5 miles and make a right turn on Route 744 and proceed to Keswick Estate entrance.

Excursions & Diversions

Both the Boar's Head Inn and Keswick Hall are conveniently located near all of the major sights and attractions. Both properties will offer suggestions to accommodate your touring needs.

The first stop on a tour through Mr. Jefferson's country is the Monticello Visitors Center at Route 20 south and I-64. The contemporary center provides an excellent introduction to the man behind the myth through four hundred artifacts, drawing models, and a film entitled *Thomas Jefferson: The Pursuit of Liberty,* shown daily. Open year round except for Christmas Day, this is also where one can purchase the Presidents Pass—admission to Monticello, James Monroe's Ash Lawn–Highland estate, and Michie Tavern.

Experienced and knowledgeable guides lead all tours through Monticello, cornerstone of Charlottesville and home to our nation's third president. Allow at least three hours for a visit that also includes the expansive gardens. Monticello, which Jefferson called his mountaintop retreat and "essay in architecture," was completely designed by him beginning in 1768. Inside the house one can enjoy seeing Jefferson's personal treasures: books, china, furniture, and some of his ingenious designs. The gardens are designed to reflect Jefferson's landscaping plans and are breathtaking in the spring when everything is in full bloom.

Jefferson's other architectural treasure is the University of Virginia, another fine example of the statesman's immense architectural talents. The Rotunda, the university's landmark structure that sits at the center of the campus, is accented by the Lawn rooms where fourth-year students, selected on merit and academic record, reside. West Range 13, a particular highlight on a stroll, is where the poet and student Edgar Allan Poe lived while attending the university. The small abode is decorated with a stuffed raven and period furnishings reflective of Poe's era.

When author William Faulkner was in residence as a visiting professor, he often walked across the Lawn, mingling with students on his way to his seminars and lectures. In fact, the university's roster of graduates echoes with the names of President Woodrow Wilson, Sen. Robert Kennedy, and author Louis Auchincloss.

Tours by students are offered daily departing from the Rotunda. Near the Rotunda is the Corner, a favorite UVA hangout where sidewalk cafes, shops and the legendary greasy spoon, White Spot, serves up Gus burgers for undergraduates on a budget.

Historic Michie Tavern, established in 1784, is another Charlottesville attraction depicting its early-American days. The tavern's dining room daily serves a buffet of fried chicken, stewed tomatoes, black-eyed peas, buttermilk biscuits, and cornbread. One can also wander through the tavern or scout out the grounds that surround the site. Montpelier, James Madison's 2,700-acre estate, is another vintage Virginia presidential home worth seeing off Route 20, as well as James Monroe's Ash Lawn–Highland estate.

Hot air ballooning has taken off in recent years as a great outing while visiting Charlottesville. With pickups available from both the Boar's Head and Keswick Hall one can fly over the many vineyards, the University of Virginia, and Monticello on a trip. The flights depart at sunrise, and the thrilling experience is followed by a champagne celebration. Albemarle County is home to many wineries and vineyards. The Jefferson Vineyards, located between Monticello and Ash Lawn, are on land once owned by Jefferson. Today one can sample and purchase a variety of selections on land that Jefferson gave to Filippo Mazzei in 1773. Oakencroft, Horton Cellars, Barboursville, and White Hall Vineyards are other top wineries worth discovering on a drive through Charlottesville and its surrounding areas.

Charlottesville Regional Chamber of Commerce

P.O. Box 1564
Charlottesville, VA 22902
Tel.: (434) 295-3144
www.cvillechamber.org

HOT SPRINGS
The Homestead

Nestled in the foothills of the Allegheny Mountains on the fringes of the lush Shenandoah Valley lies the Homestead, one of America's loveliest historic hotels, encompassing 15,000 acres and enough history to fill several notebooks.

Virginia's most historic hotel, the Homestead is a Georgian treasure whose trademark brick tower peeking through the forest recalls the grand era of the 1920s and '30s when the social elite traveled by private railroad car to the wooded Virginia resort. Opulent leisure springs to mind when touring the spacious property, listed on the National Register of Historic Places. Founded in 1766 as a health spa because of its abundance of warm mineral springs, the hotel has a sweeping veranda lined with white wicker chairs, a long-standing Homestead tradition.

Many U.S. presidents have visited and strolled its corridors, played on its golf courses, and enjoyed fly-fishing in the nearby Cascades streams. The first president to visit was Thomas Jefferson, who in 1818 rode on horseback from his home in nearby Charlottesville to visit the warm springs for their therapeutic powers. William Howard Taft, Calvin Coolidge, and Harry Truman also took advantage of the retreat to escape the pressures of the presidency.

Towering white pillars frame the sweeping lobby corridor of the Homestead in Hot Springs. *Trish Foxwell*

**North Main Street
Hot Springs, VA 24445
Tel: (540)-839-1766,
1-800-838-1766
www.thehomestead.com
$$$$
220 miles/4 hours**

Taft, like Coolidge and Hoover, enjoyed the excellent fly-fishing, and President Woodrow Wilson, accompanied by his second wife, Edith Bolling Galt, spent his honeymoon here in December 1915. Wilson, a native Virginian who grew up in Staunton, loved to take long morning walks around the property,

Franklin and Eleanor Roosevelt vacationing at the Virginia resort July 1931 while he was governor of New York. *The Homestead, Hot Springs, VA*

whereas avid golfer Dwight D. Eisenhower played endless rounds on the golf course during his presidency.

On July 4, 1931, Governor Franklin Delano Roosevelt and his wife, Eleanor, spent the Fourth of July holiday at the resort. The warm mineral springs were one major reason for Roosevelts' visit, but it was also designed as a strategy session for mapping out his successful bid for the White House.

While the Homestead can accurately be called the "resort of presidents," it has also been a haven for great golfers, captains of industry, and famous names from the movie colony. Robert Trent Jones Sr. designed and played the Lower Cascades course, and at the turn of the century many business tycoons from Wall Street flocked to the Virginia resort.

Banking financier and Wall Street millionaire J. P. Morgan had a particular fondness for the Homestead. Morgan, who spent many holidays at the hotel, was the largest single investor from the late 1800s until 1913 and was responsible for financing the Homestead's rebuilding following a disastrous fire in 1901 that destroyed the original hotel.

Morgan rebuilt the resort according to his exact specifications, adding every

One of the Homestead's financial backers, financier J.P. Morgan enjoys an afternoon garden party at the resort in 1896. *The Homestead, Hot Springs, VA*

modern convenience. Morgan, always the congenial and cordial host, loved to attend and organize extravagant garden parties, usually surrounding himself with lovely ladies and ambitious businessmen eager to discuss the latest business venture. The trademark brick tower was rebuilt and opened in 1929.

The West Wing, opened in 1904, quickly became a favorite of many prominent New York families including the Cornelius Vanderbilts, who spent their honeymoon at the resort. Mrs. Vanderbilt, always arriving by a private railroad car from New York, came to the hotel for half a century usually during the summer months to escape the steamy New York summers.

A brief dossier of other icons listed in the hotel's annals include Henry Ford, Harvey Firestone, and John D. Rockefeller, who spent as much as five weeks at the Homestead enjoying scenic mountain drives throughout the wooded property.

The Duke and Duchess of Windsor were regular guests as well, combining their lengthy stays with visits to the neighboring Greenbrier. Twelve servants and three truckloads of luggage accompanied the couple on their monthlong holiday. Being from Baltimore, the Duchess felt at home in the Virginia countryside, where friends of hers gathered for numerous social events. The couple always preferred breakfast in their suite prior to a day of entertaining. While

Mrs. Cornelius Vanderbilt, seen here circa 1938, spent 25 summers at the Virginia resort.
The Homestead, Hot Springs, VA

the Duchess planned parties for friends and guests, the Duke enjoyed hiking, swimming, and golfing during his days at the Homestead.

Wood-burning fireplaces, tea served promptly at four, guided carriage rides around the immaculately groomed golf courses, and fly-fishing at dawn are just some of the Homestead's many attractions. For those with families in tow, there are indoor and outdoor pools, a supervised children's play area, golf and tennis lessons, horseback riding, and more than a hundred miles of hiking trails.

Excursions & Diversions

The true appeal of the resort is the charming village of Hot Springs itself, a streetlong village abundant with craft shops and Sam Snead's Tavern (the golfer is from the area), whose peaceful and serene ambience is much the same as it was during the 1920s. One can step back in time and move at a more leisurely pace. There are no deadlines here except for an early morning horseback ride or teeing off at dawn.

While the era of afternoon tea dances and debutante balls has long since vanished from the hilly hideaway, civility and, above all, graciousness lies at

The Duke and Duchess of Windsor outside the Homestead circa 1940. *The Homestead, Hot Springs, VA*

the heart of the Homestead's enduring appeal. A crackling fireplace in the pillar-lined Great Hall proves an ideal place for meeting fellow guests or for sipping a glass of wine in the early evening hours. An intimate and inviting atmosphere is also found in its guest rooms, which reflect the natural beauty of the Allegheny Mountains with floral draperies and pastel chintz fabrics reminiscent of a fine Virginia manor house.

A willing and friendly activities desk staff will cater to you and streamline your visit, whether it be a weekend of golf, fly-fishing, or taking advantage of the newly remodeled and revamped spa. Falconry is another leisure pursuit that can be enjoyed at the resort, and shoppers can find an array of unique emporiums along the main hallway, and Cottage Row, just outside the Homestead, offers a variety of crafts, gifts, and books.

The resort maintains a stable of over fifty horses and offers both English- and Western-style riding. A trail ride through the forest or a carriage ride is another option on a tour. The modern equestrian center is just one of the Homestead's many spruced-up amenities. The stables feature over 11,800 square feet of hay storage, a blacksmith shop, and tack rooms. Lessons ranging from beginning to intermediate can be arranged for budding riders.

Fly-fishing requires a day permit, available at the Outpost on Cottage Row, and early reservations are recommended for this popular pastime.

The newly expanded tennis courts are also recommended. Bill Tilden, Bobby Riggs, and Helen Willis have all played at the Homestead, where eight courts provide unmatched views of the mountain setting. Golf enthusiasts can enjoy the Cascades Course, rated among the top fifty courses in the United States by *Golf Magazine*. Designed by William S. Flynn in the early 1930s, the challenging course winds its way through the Allegheny Mountains with its long narrow fairways, fast greens, and the beautiful headwaters of the Cascades' twelve waterfall streams.

The most stunning aspect of the resort is the newly renovated and expanded spa. Located where the original spa once stood, the European-style spa salon offers a variety of treatments including mineral baths fed by the Homestead's 104-degree hot springs, Swedish massages, relaxing herbal wraps, and exfoliating salt scrubs. Warm terrycloth robes make roaming around the lush enclave with its seafoam-green interior even more enjoyable.

The Homestead offers a variety of packages throughout the year aimed at couples, families, golfers, or travelers who just want to enjoy the setting. The holiday packages offered at Thanksgiving and Christmas are a particular favorite for families, and Winterfest, a food and wine weekend, is another treat for gourmets.

Owned and operated by Club Resorts, also the proprietors of Pinehurst, the Homestead has undergone a series of extensive renovations and restorations since 1995, updating the grand Virginia resort to its present Mobil Four-Star and AAA Four-Diamond status.

The Homestead

ACCOMMODATIONS: A luxury resort with 506 rooms, golf, tennis, carriage rides, fly-fishing, falconry, horseback riding and stables, indoor and outdoor pool, fitness center and European-style spa, dining.

DIRECTIONS: Take I-66 to I-81 south. Follow I-81 south to exit 240. Take Route 257 west to Route 42, then follow Route 42 south to Route 39 west to U.S. 220. Take U.S. 220 south to Hot Springs.

HUNT COUNTRY
The Red Fox Inn (Middleburg)

Mention the words "hunt country" in Virginia and images of lush, gentle hills dotted with Thoroughbred horse farms and enchanting villages steeped in Colonial and Civil War history spring to mind.

In the foothills of the Blue Ridge, Middleburg, founded in 1787 by Revolutionary War Lieutenant Col. Leven Powell, overflows with private estates and sprawling horse farms. Rolling countryside and miles of unspoiled landscape make the area a favorite of the horsey set.

The Red Fox Inn: A front view of Middleburg's most famous lodging spot. *Trish Foxwell*

2 East Washington Street
P.O. Box 385
Middleburg, VA 20118
Tel: (540) 687-6301,
**   1-800-223-1728**
www.redfoxinn.com
$$$
45 miles/1 hour

Resembling the rustic beauty of an English country village and often referred to as the "Leicestershire of America," Middleburg offers a diverse collection of shops and restaurants, not to mention a host of equine-related activities to suit weekend travelers. Once an overnight stagecoach stop midway between Alexandria and Winchester, the quiet village became the dramatic backdrop for the Gray Ghost of the Confederacy, Col. John Mosby, and his daring Mosby's Rangers.

Middleburg's appeal lies in its resplendent geographic loveliness, which is apparent as one navigates its winding country roads, and in its size. It is a village, and the residents who call this terrain home want it to remain so. It is also one of the premier horse centers in the country, ranking only behind Lexington, Kentucky, in importance among serious horse enthusiasts.

Its proximity to Washington, D.C., has also made its mark on the town. A popular weekend destination for weary Washingtonians, Middleburg has attracted presidents and diplomats alike over the years.

When President John F. Kennedy wanted to escape the pressures of the Oval Office, he and his wife, Jackie, traveled to Glen Ora, a four-hundred-acre estate far removed from the hubbub of Washington, to relax and unwind. Virginia's countryside quickly became a frequent weekend getaway for the Kennedys, particularly for Jackie , an experienced equestrian, who loved to roam and wander on horseback along private bridle paths that surrounded Glen Ora.

The late philanthropist and art collector Paul Mellon, renowned for his enormous contributions to Washington's National Gallery of Art, also fell under the hunt country spell, devoting hours to equestrian events and organizing the National Sporting Library, the largest repository on equine subjects in the United States. Paintings, rare books, and information pertaining to the horse are found in the handsome library complex.

Mellon compared the wooded domain of Upperville, where he lived, to the English countryside. His stables, Rokeby Farms, are one of the highlights on the annual Stable Hunt Country Tour. The meticulous grounds are adorned by stables and a bronze statue of Mill Reef, his beloved racehorse. Another well-known name associated with the area is Pamela Harriman, the doyenne of the Democratic social scene and former ambassador to France, who maintained a home in Middleburg prior to her death.

Long associated with the rich and famous or, as they say in these parts, the well-known and wealthy, Middleburg residents maintain low profiles for most of the year except during the fall hunts and spring races when everyone from actor Robert Duvall, who lives in the area, to the Fortune 500 crowd attend the leading equestrian events.

Recommended inns in hunt country include Middleburg's Red Fox and Goodstone Inns, Warrenton's Black Horse Inn, and the Ashby Inn in Paris. Each is unique and offers varying vistas of this picturesque region of Virginia.

The Red Fox, long the favorite of the locals and a distinguished town landmark, is the most famous of the group. Sitting in the center of town off Washington Street, the Red Fox claims important connections to both Civil War and presidential history. Billed as the "oldest original inn in America," its "lived-in look" is its inherent charm; the familiar iron jockey holding a lantern marks the way for guests.

Built in 1728 and originally called the Beveridge House, the faded brick building became a popular meeting place for Confederate general James Ewell Brown "Jeb" Stuart and Col. John Mosby and Mosby's Rangers. The Red Fox served as both a hospital and headquarters for the Virginia Confederates. In the Jeb Stuart Room, an upstairs meeting room, countless strategy sessions were conducted between the Confederate leaders while wounded soldiers were attended to and treated in the downstairs rooms.

The room also made history in the 1960s when Pierre Salinger, press secretary to President Kennedy, held impromptu press conferences and meetings when the president was in Middleburg. Pamela Harriman also made full use of the room, hosting numerous fund-raisers for Democratic candidates.

Following Kennedy's tragic assassination in 1963, Jackie, along with her children, John and Caroline, continued to visit Middleburg, attending major equestrian events or visiting her close friends, the Mellons, in Upperville. When her children got older, the former first lady opted to stay in room 33 at the McConnell House, part of the Red Fox Inn.

The expansive picture windows and four-poster bed were to her liking. The former first lady liked the fact that she could enter through the back door via the kitchen to escape the press and curious onlookers. Jackie usually spent her days in Middleburg riding, reading, and visiting the Mellons. The Virginia countryside offered her solitude and privacy. It is believed that the time she spent in the Virginia hamlet was among her happiest and most contented.

The Tavern Room, tucked behind the entrance of the lower-level dining room, was a particular favorite of the Kennedys, who always chose the table closest to the fireplace. During her marriage to Senator John Warner of Virginia, actress Elizabeth Taylor also liked the casual, cozy atmosphere of the Tavern Room, often hosting lunches for her friends while in residence.

The Red Fox abounds with charm. Fresh flowers, crackling fires, and delicious American cuisine highlight a visit. An eighteenth-century flavor is prevalent throughout, both in its dining areas and its twenty-three guest rooms, which are sprinkled throughout the four buildings that comprise the Red Fox Inn complex: the Main Inn, McConnell House, and the Stray Fox and Night Fox Inns.

The Stray Fox has eight cozy rooms complete with stenciling, plush comforters, original fireplace mantels, and antiques. Once the home of a country doctor, Robert McConnell, the Stray Fox got its name because of a misfired cannonball that struck its foundation during the Civil War.

The wood-paneled dining room with its fireplace is a favorite during the

Thanksgiving and Christmas holiday season, when turkey with all the trimmings is served Colonial style. Open year round, the Red Fox continues to be a favorite "coach stop" for travelers wishing to get a genuine taste of Virginia's hunt country and possibly a glimpse of someone famous.

The Red Fox Inn

ACCOMMODATIONS: Country inn with twenty-three rooms, each with private bath, cable TV. Dining room.

DIRECTIONS: Head out Route 50 west from the Washington Beltway. The Red Fox is in the center of Middleburg on your right, approximately one hour's drive from Washington.

The Goodstone Inn (Middleburg)

On any given morning as a mist gently drapes the verdant landscape, a red fox or rider on horseback might be spotted outside windows at the posh and ultraplush Goodstone Inn. The most luxurious and newest of the restored inns on the Middleburg scene, the Goodstone, which has been winning accolades since its opening in 1998, is the closest thing to staying in an elegant Middleburg country estate without having to actually buy one.

Secluded and serene, the Goodstone is situated on 285 acres of prime real estate down a twisting mountain road abundant with meadows and farmland. Resembling a country estate more than a former carriage house and stables, the inn has thirteen guest rooms in four distinctive buildings scattered throughout its wooded property.

The barn doors outside Hunt Country's luxurious Goodstone Inn. *Trish Foxwell*

36205 Snake Hill Rd.
Middleburg, VA 20117
Tel: (540) 687-4645
** 1-877-219-4663**
www.goodstoneinn.com
$$$$
47 miles/1 hour

The Main House or Carriage House, with its soft green hues and large Palladian windows, is where breakfast, tea, and Sunday brunch are served. It is the inn's main social gathering place and is the place to arrange any number of activities ranging from golf to canoeing and riding expeditions. It is joined by the outlying buildings of the Dutch Cottage, Spring House, and French Farm Cottage, which round out the property.

The rural ambience is inviting with its rocking chairs on porches, scrumptious Belgian waffles served at breakfast, and wondrous views of Virginia's countryside and the Blue Ridge Mountains. The most unique accommodations are found in the former stable area that flanks the main house.

For avid equestrians, staying in the former barn and stall area is irresistible. The room's long and narrow proportions and its pictures of hunt and horse scenes add to the homey atmosphere. Visitors can almost imagine their quarter horse or Thoroughbred bunking down beside them for the night in the accommodations, which are a favorite for families. The two-bedroom Dutch Cottage with its own fireplace, sitting room, and kitchen is ideal for families, while the three-bedroom French Farm offers an open kitchen, vaulted living room, and floor-to-ceiling stone fireplace.

Only minutes from town, the Goodstone has a rich pedigree including both Revolutionary and Civil War history. In 1768 "Jamie the Scot" Leith settled in the area to purchase a plantation. From his original 640-acre tract of land, Leith supplied stores and provisions to the Continental army. In 1915, following several ownerships, the Goodwin family bought the land and renamed it the Goodstone. All that remained of the original site was an ivy-covered facade that overlooks the mansion pool.

Frederick Warburg, a member of a prominent and wealthy New York banking family responsible for financing the Harriman railroads, purchased the property in 1943 and added a swimming pool, bathhouse, and arbors. Renaming the property Snake Hill Farm, the Warburgs used the house as a second home during the fall hunts.

A major restoration and redesigning took place in 1996 shortly after the Warburgs sold the property. Since 1998 the inn has been privately owned and operated and offers luxurious accommodations in a woodsy setting complete with four-poster beds, horse scenes, and a range of outdoor activities that can be scheduled through its accommodating staff. The inn can arrange horseback riding through a neighboring barn and stables.

The Goodstone Inn

ACCOMMODATIONS: Luxurious country inn with thirteen rooms. Room rates include breakfast, afternoon tea, and a fully stocked bar in every room. Dining room, pool, hot tub, mountain biking.

DIRECTIONS: Take Route 50 west into Middleburg. Look for the stoplight in the center of the village and take a right onto North Madison Street (Red Fox Inn is on the right before you turn onto North Madison Street). Bear right around the Y in the road and continue north and go past the Middleburg Elementary School, which you will see on your right. Travel straight to Foxcroft Road for about 2.5 miles, crossing over Benton's Bridge. After you have crossed the bridge, take the first left onto Snake Hill Road, travel 300 yards, and look to your left for the Goodstone Inn.

The Black Horse Inn (Warrenton)

Another great lodging option in hunt country is the Black Horse Inn in Warrenton. A horse-country estate, the original part of the inn was built prior to the Civil War and named after the Black Horse Cavalry, which led a successful charge against Union troops during the First Battle of Manassas.

Horses graze outside Warrenton's inviting Black Horse Inn. *Courtesy of Black Horse Inn*

Known as Company H of the Fourth Virginia Cavalry, the unit became a scouting team and bodyguard for Gen. Stonewall Jackson and Gen. Joseph E. Johnson. The mystique of cavalry officers riding on horseback atop the hill to the inn prevails today where horses grazing on the hillside, plush four-poster canopied beds, and Civil War remnants remind visitors of Virginia's Civil War history.

8393 Meetze Road
Warrenton, VA 20187
Tel: (540) 349-4020
www.blackhorseinn.com
$$$
45 miles/1 hour

The inn has nine distinctive rooms all furnished with period antiques and reproductions recalling Virginia's Old South heritage. Hunter's Haven, located in the oldest part of the inn, reveals a masculine décor with an exposed-rock fireplace, four-poster Chippendale canopy bed, and hunting lodge ambience. Reynards Retreat is one of the Black Horse Inn's most comfortable and elegant rooms. A queen-sized four-poster bed and fox-themed atmosphere are found in this cozy corner of the inn. The Jeffersonian Suite, a second-floor corner room, is reminiscent of Monticello's bedrooms, complete with a hand-carved four-poster bed and oversized claw-foot tub and shower.

The bridal suite, aptly called Great Expectations, is romantic and airy. Here a working fireplace, separate sun porch, and spacious dressing room can be enjoyed. The inn, situated on twenty acres, proves an ideal setting for weddings where a horse-drawn carriage transports the couple to the Gilded Fox, the reception facility.

A Continental breakfast is served at the inn, and a variety of excellent restaurants are located nearby for dinner and lunch, including the Rail Stop in

The Plains and the Inn at Little Washington, a renowned Mobil Five-Star restaurant specializing in European fare.

A variety of recreational activities can be enjoyed while visiting the Black Horse including jogging along nearby trails, tennis, canoeing, golfing at three nearby courses, and horseback riding.

The Black Horse Inn

ACCOMMODATIONS: Country inn with eight newly restored period rooms, each with a private bath; some with fireplaces and Jacuzzi. Room rate includes Continental breakfast.

DIRECTIONS: The Black Horse Inn is 45 miles southwest of Washington at the intersection of Routes 29 and 643. From Washington take Route 66 west to exit 43A, marked Route 29 South, Gainesville. Continue on Route 29 south for 10.5 miles and bear left toward Culpeper/Fredericksburg. Take the second exit to Old Town Warrenton marked Warrenton, Route 643—Meetze Road. Turn left on Route 643, and the Black Horse Inn is located 1.6 miles on the left-hand side of the road.

The Ashby Inn (Paris)

Twelve miles west of Middleburg in the tiny hamlet of Paris (population 50), the Ashby Inn awaits visitors who want to walk through history and experience fine dining without the crowds.

Described as "a great restaurant with rooms," the Ashby Inn has four guest rooms in the School House building and six rooms in the main inn—both reflecting the décor and ambience of the eighteenth century. From George Washington, who mentioned the Ashby Tavern in his diaries, to John Singleton Mosby, the Gray Ghost of the Confederacy, the village has played an important part in American Colonial and Civil War history.

Innkeepers Roma and John Sherman have successfully combined a great dining spot with an array of lovely appointed rooms where wood-burning fireplaces, oriental rugs, four-poster beds, and private porches with comfortable Adirondack chairs and commanding views of the Blue Ridge afford

Ashby Inn: Chairs adorn the relaxing porch area at the Ashby Inn.
Ashby Inn

692 Federal Street
Paris, VA 20130
Tel: (540) 592-3900
www.ashbyinn.com
60 miles/1¼ hours

travelers a genuine taste of "old Virginia." The inn, which opened in 1984, has four distinctive dining rooms that range from banquettes to the original kitchen with a fireplace and full-service bar. The patio reveals panoramic views of the Blue Ridge. The inn's varied menu usually highlights a particular season.

The area abounds in Civil War sites, hiking trails along the famed Appalachian Trail, as well as hunt country activities in the neighboring towns of Middleburg, The Plains, and Leesburg. Part of the joy in visiting this charming establishment is the genuine hospitality of John and Roma Sherman, who truly make every guest feel at home. The scrumptious cooking is worth the visit to this enchanting hideaway that sometimes gets overlooked in favor of the neighboring inns. The tiny town of Paris adds to a visit. If your heart desires a country retreat accompanied by great cooking and exceptional hospitality, a visit to the Ashby should be at the top of your list!

The Ashby Inn and Restaurant

ACCOMMODATIONS: Intimate country inn with six guest rooms each with private bath. Excellent dining rooms.

DIRECTIONS: Paris lies about 60 miles west of Washington, DC, at the intersection of Routes 17 and 50. From the Washington Beltway take Route 66 west to exit 23 (Delaplane/Paris), continue 7.5 miles north on Route 17, and then turn left on Route 701, which runs directly into the village.

Excursions & Diversions

All things equine are on the activities list on a swing through hunt country. Throughout the year myriad events are held in the region. Middleburg's Farmers Market, held from May through October at the Middleburg Community Center, is a local favorite for buying fresh farm goods and flowers. This is an ideal place for rubbing shoulders with the locals and for finding out what's new in town.

The Hunt Country Stable Tour, usually held the last weekend in May, is a must for horse enthusiasts. Sponsored by Upperville's Trinity Episcopal Church, the self-guided driving tour showcases the magnificent horse farms in hunt country. The tour allows visitors a rare opportunity to peek behind the gates of some of the area's finest horse farms.

The Virginia Gold Cup, a premier equestrian sporting event, is a chance to see exceptional steeplechase races at the Great Meadows Events Center in The Plains. The race takes place the first Saturday in May. Horses competing in the prestigious and popular event travel from around the globe. The 1911 landmark Glenwood Park is another great spot, especially in the fall when jumpers compete in the annual classic. Picnics, tailgate parties, and lots of champagne and Virginia wine can be enjoyed at this popular event.

At Middleburg Training Center, a Thoroughbred training center, one can see those gorgeous racehorses being groomed and trotted around the course for early-morning workouts. Open year round, a visit to the center is a treat for camera buffs desiring to catch streamlined racehorses in action.

One of Middleburg's newest attractions is the National Sporting Library, which offers visitors one of the most comprehensive collections relating to horses in the nation. Paintings, bronze sculptures, special exhibits, seminars, and a research library are among the resources available in this attractive setting. Donated to Middleburg by Paul Mellon, this lovely research library has been rated the best in the nation for gathering information regarding horses.

Dog Days at Oatlands in nearby Leesburg is another crowd-pleaser. The two-day canine festival features man's best friend in sheepdog trials. Sheepdogs demonstrate their unique skills in this popular and fun-filled event, which is a favorite for families. Food and craft items are offered for sale. Expect large crowds at this annual spring event.

Loudoun County Visitors Association

222 Catoctin Circle, SE
Suite 100
Leesburg, VA 20175-3730
Tel: (703) 771-2617; 1-800-752-6118
www.visitloudoun.org

RICHMOND
The Jefferson Hotel

A city whose destiny and heritage were largely shaped by Civil War heroes and tobacco barons, Virginia's capital city, lined with historic districts and overlooking the rock-strewn James River, is where one will find the stately and exquisite Jefferson Hotel, Virginia's only AAA Five-Diamond and Mobil Five-Star hotel. The Jefferson tells the Richmond story like no other landmark in the city.

Richmond, founded by Captains Christopher Newport and John Smith in 1607, was also the capital of the Confederacy during the Civil War when the battle cry "On to Richmond" became the slogan of the Union troops in defeating the South. But Civil War history is only one facet of Richmond's illustrious and tumultuous past. Tobacco money built the many great mansions that stretch along Monument Avenue, and literary genius Edgar Allan Poe first made his mark in the city that became so important in his later years. Richmond also boasts one of the finest collections of Fabergé's jewel-encrusted creations outside Russia, and tennis great Arthur Ashe went on to win Wimbledon following his Richmond youth.

The Jefferson Hotel: Richmond's Franklin Street entrance to the Mobil Five-Star Jefferson Hotel.
Trish Foxwell

101 West Franklin Street
Richmond, VA 23220
Tel: (804) 788-8000;
1-800-424-8014
www.jefferson-hotel.com
$$$$
100 miles/2 hours

Most of Richmond's history can be traced at the Jefferson Hotel, Richmond's most revered architectural gem, which was saved from destruction in recent years, giving the downtown area a much-needed economic boost and revitalization.

Visiting the Jefferson is alone worth the trip to Richmond. The hotel's annals read like a list from "Who's Who in American History." From the moment you step inside the hotel's dazzling interior where Tiffany windows and a commanding statue of Thomas Jefferson greet you, you are reminded of Richmond's stature and the integral part it played during the Civil War.

The Jefferson was the daring and costly dream of Maj. Lewis Gintner, a visionary and one of Richmond's wealthiest tobacco barons. who envisioned his monumental palace to be "the finest hotel the city had ever seen." The Beaux Arts structure displays Renaissance touches throughout its interior where cathedral ceilings and intricate woodwork accentuate its European atmosphere.

Gintner was no different from other newly minted turn-of-the-century millionaires who desired to build living legacies as testimony to their vast wealth. He spared no expense in carrying out his ambitious dream. Employing the architectural talents of Carrere and Hastings, Gintner launched his bold mission in 1893. Cost was no object to the millionaire, who wanted only the finest things that money could buy for his hotel.

Costs estimated to be between $5 million and $10 million did not deter Gintner from completing his ambitious plan. Items imported from around the globe were delivered to the Jefferson Hotel daily, ultimately making it Richmond's most prized architectural treasure. The Palm Court with its exotic plants exhibited the fashion of the flamboyant Gilded Age, with rare antiques and priceless artifacts lending to its glamorous atmosphere. Every luxury of the period was carefully incorporated in the Jefferson's overall design, from a gentlemen's billiards room to a well-stocked library. A tea court was also put into place for its inherent genteel appeal. The Jefferson was also one of the first hotels to install electric lights and elevators, making it not only Richmond's most elegant building but also its most modern.

The Richmond millionaire wanted the hotel's opening night to be the splashiest that Richmond society had ever seen. On Halloween eve 1895, Gintner got his long-awaited wish. Fancy carriages lined up for miles along Franklin Street, dispatching elegantly attired guests into the hotel. The spotlight was on Gintner and his magnificent creation. His enchanted evening became the talk of the town; a party for three hundred guests was held in the Main Ballroom. But the evening's most coveted social event took place in the Roof Garden, where New York architect Stanford White threw a lavish party for the lovely Richmond debutante Irene Langhorne and her dashing fiancé, Charles Dana Gibson of Gibson Girl fame.

Overnight the Jefferson became a sensation and a legend was born. Things would never be the same in the Southern city that instantaneously had transformed itself from a remnant of its Civil War past into a symbol of the renascent South. Fine shops and cafés soon dotted the downtown area, and trains transported guests to the opulent downtown hotel from Washington, Philadelphia, and New York.

In 1907 another of Richmond's most famous inhabitants was born. The Jefferson would play a key role in the life of Bill "Bojangles" Robinson. The gifted tap dancer, who went on to star in Vaudeville and Hollywood, got his start at the Jefferson. Bojangles got a job in the hotel's dining room, hoping to be discovered by a New York producer. The aspiring dancer, who often danced on the sidewalks of Richmond to show off his immense talent, got his big break one night when a producer from Hollywood was dining at the Jefferson. Word got out that Abe Fortner was in town, and Robinson offered to work that evening. The story goes that Robinson "accidentally" spilled oyster stew on Fortner and danced his way to the kitchen to show off his tap-dancing prowess. Robinson's plan worked, and the next day Fortner offered the dancer money to get to New York. Shortly thereafter, Bojangles headed to New York and eventually to Hollywood, where he starred with Shirley Temple in *The Little Colonel*. Bojangles and Fortner remained lifelong friends. When Robinson returned to Richmond on occasional visits in his later years, he would stop in at the hotel that had changed his life.

While many of the hotel's records have been lost or destroyed over the years, the ones that remain reveal an enviable list of luminaries. Everyone from Charles Lindbergh to Charlie Chaplin, Elvis Presley, and Frank Sinatra has stayed at the Jefferson. In recent years actors Diane Keaton, Jack Lemmon, and Warren Beatty have been guests.

One of the more captivating stories about the Jefferson dates back to 1927 when Charles Lindbergh attended a dinner in his honor at the hotel. The handsome young aviator dined and danced in the hotel's ballroom while fans jammed the balcony to the rafters in the hopes of catching a glimpse of him.

Following the Jefferson's illustrious Gilded Age, it hosted a parade of celebrities, film stars, and dignitaries throughout the 1920s and early '30s. Charlie Chaplin, stage actress Sarah Bernhardt, and Scott and Zelda Fitzgerald were some of the names associated with that era. Chaplin always preferred suites on his travels, and the Jefferson staff catered to every need of the adored "Little Tramp." Author Thomas Wolfe stopped off on his train trips from New York to Asheville.

Archival photo of Elvis at the Jefferson. *Photo courtesy of the Jefferson Hotel*

Elvis Presley's visit in 1956 took the hotel by storm. On the brink of super-stardom, Elvis was in Richmond for a performance. Arriving by cab at the Jefferson, the rock and roll heartthrob with the raven-black hair and infectious smile strutted to the front desk. With his transistor radio playing rock and roll music. Elvis registered at the hotel. His coffee shop visit the next day caused quite a stir and is recounted at the hotel to this day. Sitting at the counter, the friendly singer, accompanied by a pretty blonde attired in rhinestone earrings and a black chemise, quietly ate a lunch of chili while conversing with the waitress.

Shortly after the visit by Elvis, the Jefferson suffered an economic downturn. With the city undergoing racial strife and many residents moving to the suburbs, the hotel finally closed its doors in 1980. The "Belle of the 1890s" that had catered to the carriage trade in the Gilded Age, countless presidents, celebrities, and the king of rock and roll, had become a tired remnant of Richmond's past.

After a 1901 fire, the hotel was restored, but to many area residents, it seemed the Jefferson had been in a steady decline since its second fire in 1944. Efforts to revive the aging dowager began in 1983 when more than $34 million was invested to begin the Jefferson's initial restoration.

Reopened in 1986 under the Sheraton name, the Jefferson was on its way to recapturing its former glory, but the arduous task of restoring a building that had sadly become the white elephant on Franklin Street became a costly endeavor. The mammoth project involved cleaning the stained-glass windows in the Palm Court, refurbishing marble floors ,and peeling off layers and layers of paint that had been applied to the original mahogany paneling.

Many of Richmond's residents came to the rescue and returned many of the items that had been sold at auctions. Hand-carved fireplace mantels, elaborate ceiling fixtures, and antique wall sconces were resurrected from the hotel's attic, all with the hope of restoring the hotel's original beauty.

In July 1991 another $5 million restoration took place when the hotel was sold to its present owners, Richmond businessman William H. Goodwin Jr. and Beverly W. Armstrong, under the company name of Historic Hotels, LLC. Under the Historic Hotels reign, the Jefferson now displays a redesigned courtyard entrance, an indoor swimming pool, and redecorated guest rooms that are constantly being upgraded. Lemaire, its AAA Five-Diamond restaurant since 1996, features American and Continental cuisine. Ongoing refurbishments help maintain the hotel's exacting standards.

The rotunda, clearly the Jefferson's striking centerpiece, with its soaring ceilings embellished with gold-leaf designs and motifs and a multicolored skylight, shines and sparkles like never before. The statue of Thomas Jefferson sculpted by Edward Valentine, one of the hotel's most priceless possessions, once again stands like a proud and vigilant sentinel over Richmond's most revered landmark and one of Virginia's most treasured architectural jewels.

The Jefferson Hotel

ACCOMMODATIONS: An elegant city hotel with 260 rooms, 40 suites, indoor pool, fitness center, and complimentary shuttle van and town car for trips within a three-mile radius of the hotel. Fine dining rooms.

DIRECTIONS: Follow I-95 South to Richmond, take exit 76B (Belvedere Street). Turn left on Leigh Street, then right onto Belvedere Street. At the fifth light, turn left onto Franklin Street. The hotel is four blocks down, on the right.

Excursions & Diversions

The Mobil Five-Star Jefferson will tailor your visit to suit your needs. One convenient service is the complimentary shuttle and limousine town car that will carry you to sites within a three-mile radius of the hotel. Some recommended sites served by the hotel that should not be overlooked include the Poe Museum, St. John's Church, the Museum of the Confederacy, the Virginia Museum of Fine Arts, and the Virginia Historical Society.

Shockoe Slip, another restoration project, is a great place to walk and explore the Edgar Allan Poe Museum. Dedicated to Richmond's most celebrated literary figure, the museum's complex consists of five buildings with the central building being one of the oldest structures in Richmond. Inside the museums one can learn more about Poe and his writings. This is one of the finest collections of Poe memorabilia in the country. First editions, manuscripts, letters, and personal artifacts belonging to the poet make a visit an exciting endeavor for literary buffs. The heart of the museum is the Old Stone House. Opened in 1922, this is an ideal place to begin your Poe journey.

Poe's attachment to Richmond was a lifelong one. He grew up in the city and married here, and his mother is buried at St. John's Church Cemetery. The museum staff will guide you and offer a great deal of information detailing Poe's creative life.

The Museum and White House of the Confederacy houses the nation's most comprehensive collection of political and military artifacts associated with the Civil War. Letters, old uniforms, weapons, and other artifacts adorn its interior. Another recommended Civil War site on Richmond's Civil War Trail is the Civil War Center at the Tredegar Iron Works near the canal. The Richmond

Civil War Trail map is available through the Richmond Convention and Visitors Bureau, where a detailed guide points out the major points of Civil War history in Richmond.

The Virginia Museum of Fine Arts is a must on a Richmond tour. It houses an outstanding collection of Art Nouveau, Art Deco, and Impressionist paintings. The most stunning galleries are Paul Mellon's British Sporting Paintings and the breathtaking Fabergé collection—the largest public display outside Russia. To anyone with an interest in the genius jeweler this is an exceptional treat. The Imperial Easter eggs, enameled photograph frames, cigarette cases, and delicately designed artifacts make this gallery a scene-stealer. Plan on spending at least half a day here where a café, bookshop, and lovely garden area will enhance your outing.

The "story of Virginia" can be enjoyed at the nearby Virginia Historical Society and Museum. A Conestoga wagon, vintage Richmond streetcar, and buttons from Pocahontas's hat are highlights of the extensive collection.

St. John's Church, Richmond's most historic church, built in 1714, is where Patrick Henry delivered his passionate speech, "Give me liberty or give me death." Other interesting neighborhoods worth exploring on a swing through Richmond include Carytown, filled with eclectic shops and restaurants, and Jackson Ward, neighborhood of Bojangles and other important African Americans. The Black History Museum and Cultural Center depicts African American life in the Old Dominion from Jamestown until today. White-water rafting trips on the James River can also be enjoyed, and Belle Isle, within the city limits, is a prime birding area. Farther afield is the Lewis Gintner Botanical Garden, a twenty-five-acre woodland garden showcasing spring flowers, which rounds out Richmond's many attractions.

Richmond Metropolitan Convention and Visitors Bureau

401 N. 3rd Street
Richmond, VA 23219
1-888-RICHMOND
www.richmondva.org

ROANOKE
The Hotel Roanoke

Fashioned after the great railway hotels of Europe, the Hotel Roanoke, just over the hill from the Homestead, was the creation of Frederick Kimball, president of the Shenandoah Valley Railroad, who formed the Norfolk & Western Railroad.

The Hotel Roanoke: A panoramic view of the Roanoke Valley's Hotel Roanoke. *The Hotel Roanoke & Conference Center*

Kimball ingeniously connected the rail lines leading north to south and east to west with Roanoke at its center, ultimately leading to the city's growth.

Roanoke, originally called Big Lick, became a thriving railroad crossroads because of Kimball's vision. If the railway was responsible for bringing commerce into Roanoke, it was the hotel that paved the way for tourism and travelers.

Stepping inside the grand old Tudor Revival building offers rare glimpses into

110 Shenandoah Ave.
Roanoke, VA 24016
Tel: (540) 985-5900
1-866-594-4722
www.hotelroanoke.com
$$$
251 miles /4 hours

Roanoke's railroad legacy and strategic location in the South. The original hotel, constructed in 1882, was a rambling wooden structure offering fewer than a dozen rooms for travelers. The oldest remaining portion was built in 1931. Surviving a catastrophic fire in 1898, the Great Depression, and the economic effects of two world wars, the hotel became the hub of Roanoke society during the 1930s and '40s. The train station that once stood at its doorstep brought travelers en route to Florida during the winter season, making it a popular stopping-off point. Even during the Great Depression in 1931, the railroad spent $225,000 for a wing with seventy-five rooms and a sixty-car garage.

During World War II, with U.S. Navy fliers training in Roanoke, the Pine Room became a makeshift officers' club and the train depot became an embarking point for hundreds of soldiers heading off to war in Europe and the Pacific.

The 332-room hotel, which added a new wing in 1955, underwent a series of economic downturns that finally led to its closing in 1989, when the Norfolk &

Southern Railroad shut down the hotel and donated it to the Virginia Tech Real Estate Foundation. Reopened in 1995, the hotel to date has spent $28 million in restoring the treasured landmark to its original luster.

Listed on the National Register of Historic Places, the Hotel Roanoke now features a state-of-the-art conference center. Operated by the Doubletree brand of Hilton Hotels, the hotel and conference center is a joint project of Hotel Roanoke, the city of Roanoke, and Virginia Tech.

The Tudor Revival entrance, tower, and two wings date back to 1938.

Debutante balls, society cotillions, and many Virginia Tech dances have graced its ballrooms through the years.

Once entirely clad in Virginia creeper, the Hotel Roanoke has witnessed a host of famous faces throughout its history. William Jennings Bryan, Amelia Earhart, Van Cliburn, Nelson Rockefeller, J. P. Morgan, and Gerald Ford, who visited while vice president in 1974, are just some of the names on its roster.

One of the hotel's shining moments occurred in 1964 when gospel singer Mahalia Jackson while on tour became the first African American to stay at the hotel. This led the way for other southern hotels to follow suit.

The Hotel Roanoke underwent another major facelift in 2001 when all of the public areas and guest rooms were remodeled. Touches of the old and new can be found. New carpets, draperies, and upgraded furniture with a Colonial décor make the hotel once again Roanoke's most important architectural landmark.

The AAA Four-Diamond hotel has not forgotten its past. In its award-winning Regency Dining Room one can still get former Chef Fred Brown's renowned peanut soup and delicious Virginia ham dishes.

The original Czech-made crystal chandeliers that were once part of the ballroom are now in the conference center, and the Pine Room has been beautifully reinstated as the hotel's casual gathering place.

The Hotel Roanoke

ACCOMMODATIONS: City hotel with 332 rooms incuding suites. Fitness center and pool. Two dining rooms and Palm Court serving morning coffee and afternoon tea.

DIRECTIONS: From I-81 South take exit 143 (I-581 South) to exit 5. Bear right onto Wells Avenue; parking is straight ahead.

Excursions & Diversions

The Market Square Bridge connects the Hotel Roanoke and Conference Center to all of the major downtown attractions.

Art galleries, shops, restaurants, and the farmers' market are a sampling of diversions found in this southern Virginia town.

The Roanoke Valley, a shining star of the Blue Ridge, is recognized for its rich railroad heritage. The newly remodeled Virginia Museum of Transportation is home to the largest collection of diesel and steam locomotives in the United States, including the Class J no. 611 steam engine and over fifty pieces of rolling stock in the museum's rail yard. This is one of the best railroad museums in the country and a must on a Roanoke tour. Antique cars, carriages, buses, and trolleys are also part of the prized collection, which attracts rail buffs from around the country.

The Science Museum of Western Virginia on Market Square offers hands-on exhibits, planetarium shows, and exhibit galleries exploring the physics of light, sound, weather, and geology. Farmers Market at Center in the Square is a Roanoke landmark dating back to 1882 when licenses were issued to twenty-five hucksters. Today this bustling shopping area offers produce markets, art galleries, country stores, and restaurants. Studios-in-the-Square is another Roanoke highlight and is recommended for art aficionados. Here original arts and crafts from Virginia's finest artisans can be found.

Roanoke hosts an array of special events throughout the year. The Festival in the Park is one of its most-attended events. The annual eleven-day celebration at the end of May includes visual and performing arts along with sporting events. The Taste of the Blue Ridge Blues and Jazz Festival is another crowd-pleaser. Staged in September, the premier food and music festival features national and international blues and jazz artists. At Christmas, "Dickens of a Christmas" is presented the first three Friday evenings in December. The Victorian celebration includes caroling, storytelling, and horse-drawn carriage rides throughout downtown Roanoke.

Outdoor activities also abound in this corner of Virginia. The Appalachian Trail winds its way through the Roanoke Valley as part of the George Washington and Jefferson National Forests, offering fly-fishing, biking, hiking, and birding. Comfortable day trips from the Hotel Roanoke include the Booker T. Washington National Monument in Hardy, Virginia, which pays tribute to one of America's most influential African Americans. The National D-Day Memorial in Bedford recognizes the town that suffered more casualties per capita on D-Day than any other town in the country. An English garden, invasion tableau, and victory arch pay homage to the valiant Virginia men who lost their lives June 6, 1944.

Roanoke Valley Convention and Visitors Bureau

114 Market St.
Roanoke, VA 24011-1402
Tel: (540) 342-6025; 1-800-635-5535
www.visitroanokeva.com

VIRGINIA BEACH
The Cavalier Hotel

Virginia Beach's oldest hotel, the Cavalier, dates back to May 9, 1926, when the cornerstone of the massive brick building was put into place.

In a city that has become Virginia's fastest growing, the Cavalier recalls another era when the sleepy seaport city was all the rage for the big bands of the 1940s.

Building the towering brick structure (500,000 bricks were used in the construction) cost over $2 million. It took 225 men thirteen months of steady labor to complete the arduous construction task. With the determination of 300 local businessmen who envisioned the potential of a beachside resort, the Cavalier was born.

The hotel's site overlooking the Atlantic Ocean and originally encompassing 250 acres added to its initial allure and aura. Soon enjoying the reputation as the "Aristocrat of the Virginia Seashore," the Cavalier was a hotel of firsts. A stock brokerage firm located on the lower-lobby level had a ticker tape directly from Wall Street, ensuring that guests could keep track of their investments while on holiday. A beauty parlor, barbershop, and a host of trendy shops rounded out its lower enclave. Golf, tennis, and swimming along with both beachside and formal dining rooms made the hotel Virginia Beach's most luxurious.

From April 4 to April 9, 1927, weeklong festivities introduced the Cavalier to the world, and with the hotel's opening came a rush of tourists to the exclusive Virginia seaside resort. Presidents, senators, and dashing young

The Cavalier Hotel: Flowers and pastel colors adorn the lobby of Virginia Beach's historic Cavalier Hotel. *Cavalier Hotel*

Oceanfront at 42nd St.
Virginia Beach, VA 23451
1-800-446-8199
www.cavalierhotel.com
$$$
215 miles/3¾ hours

naval officers, who frequently traveled from nearby Norfolk to enjoy the inviting atmosphere, made the hotel a social meeting place from the onset. Many of the South's finest families spent weeks, not days, at the posh Virginia resort. The Cavalier's innovative amenities included four water lines installed in every guest room offering hot, cold, salt, and ice water.

In 1927 Mayor S. Heth Tyler became the first American to congratulate aviator Charles Lindbergh via radio broadcast from the hotel as he passed over the old Cape Henry Lighthouse following his historic transatlantic flight.

Trains from the Midwest and the North soon carried guests to the resort, which in a few short years had become Virginia's finest. In time the Cavalier attracted Hollywood's elite, prime ministers, U.S. presidents, and diplomats, who often traveled from Washington to enjoy the summer sun.

Opened on Memorial Day 1929, the Beach Club added another dimension to the Cavalier's appeal. During the 1930s and '40s the club, which was initially private, attracted the best bands of the Big Band era. Famous musicians of the day including Benny Goodman, Glenn Miller, Tommy Dorsey, Cab Calloway, Guy Lombardo, Lawrence Welk, and Frank Sinatra all played at the Cavalier. Bing Crosby, who played with Lawrence Welk's singing trio, the Rhythm Boys, can also be added to the roster of notable entertainers. Swinging big-band music could be heard for miles around, adding to the Cavalier's swanky reputation. An invitation to the Beach Club became the most coveted in town.

Carlos Wilson, official historian of the Cavalier and onetime busboy, fondly recalls the visits of other notables including Elizabeth Taylor, Bette Davis, Jean Harlow, Judy Garland, Betty Grable, who accompanied her bandleader husband Harry James, and Eleanor Roosevelt, who arrived with a group of Girl Scouts. President Richard Nixon loved the roaring fireplace in the Hunt Room. Other presidents listed in the hotel's annals include Calvin Coolidge, Herbert Hoover, Harry Truman, Dwight Eisenhower, and John Kennedy.

From 1942 to 1945 the Cavalier was converted into military barracks for throngs of naval officers arriving in Norfolk during World War II. The Navy leased the hotel as a radar training school. During this period the Cavalier's appearance changed dramatically. Blackout curtains were placed over the indoor pool's windows, and water was drained from the swimming pool to aid in the naval training maneuvers. The once glistening lobby had become a tired and tarnished remnant. The Virginia Beach landmark where the big bands had once played was off limits during the war years as surveillance planes hovered overhead. Rumors quickly spread that the hotel was finished, its glory days behind it. The Cavalier, which had played such a key role during World War II, finally closed its doors in 1973. A year later, in October 1974, a group of local schoolchildren came to the rescue and started a "Save the Cavalier" campaign. With their ardent fundraising and the help of area businesses, the hotel was saved from the wrecking ball. In 1976, following a series of million-dollar renovations, the hotel reopened for the summer months, eventually leading the way for its present year-round operation.

In 1973 the spanking-new Cavalier Oceanfront opened to the public. Eleven stories high, the modern hotel became the beachfront part of the older Cavalier Hotel.

Today ongoing renovations keep the Cavalier's reputation for poise and polish intact. Honoring this revered Virginia Beach landmark and the glamour of its earlier days, a series of renovations for its private and public areas is planned. The entire northwest wing has been remodeled, new carpeting and drapes have been installed in most of the guest rooms, and plans at press time are to revitalize its dining rooms.

Privately owned since 1959 by Glen Dixon, the property presently sits on eighteen acres of Virginia Beach oceanfront encompassing the original Cavalier Hotel (now known as Cavalier on the Hill) and the Cavalier Oceanfront. The two hotels offer a combined total of four hundred guest rooms and twenty-two suites, five restaurants, tennis courts, bike rental facilities, and Olympic-sized swimming pools. The newer eleven-story oceanfront hotel offers the finest in beachfront accommodations. One can rent a cabana for the day or opt for a bike ride along the boardwalk.

The Hunt Room with its gargantuan fireplace is open from January through April. A favorite winter haunt for the locals, marshmallows and roasting sticks are a winter tradition. Large, overstuffed chairs in front of the fireplace remind guests of the hotel's golden past. Orion's, the signature seafood restaurant atop the Cavalier Oceanfront, offers unparalleled views of the Atlantic Ocean. One might almost hear the big bands of yesteryear while dining in this spectacular setting.

Excursions & Diversions

Although the inviting Atlantic Ocean waterfront is a compelling magnet for swimmers, surfers, and sailors on a Virginia Beach outing, the Tidewater is endowed with a wide range of diverse cultural and outdoor activities worth exploring and enjoying.

The U.S. Fish & Wildlife's Back Bay National Wildlife Refuge is within easy reach of the Cavalier. Located approximately twenty minutes from the hotel south of Sandbridge on Sandpiper Road, the refuge, which encompasses 8,000 acres of wild terrain, is situated on a pristine strip of land typical of barrier islands found along the Eastern Seaboard.

No fewer than ten thousand snow geese and a large variety of ducks pass over during the peak fall migration in December, making the refuge a birder's haven. Marshlands, fields, woodlands, and farmlands make the wildlife habitat one of Virginia's most captivating. Raptors, rabbits, red fox, loggerhead sea turtles, and deer are common at Back Bay.

Nearly three hundred species of birds have been recorded at Back Bay, including sandpipers, warblers, tundra swans, bald eagles, peregrine falcons, and piping plovers. During the winter season wildlife photographers gather at the refuge in the hopes of gathering unforgettable images of its wildlife. In addition to birding, which is exceptional here, there are abundant hiking trails and fishing areas. A visitors center displays the latest wildlife spottings as well as detailed trail maps that give the general lay of the land.

Within a thirty-minute drive from the Cavalier on I-64 heading north is the Chrysler Museum of Art. Rated one of the nation's finest, the museum, founded in 1939 as the Norfolk Museum of Arts and Sciences, became world renowned when automobile magnate Walter Chrysler presented Norfolk with his vast private art collection of American and European art.

Facing the Hague River inlet of Norfolk's Elizabeth River, the museum houses sixty stunning galleries, an auditorium, a dazzling gift shop, a restaurant, and the Jean Oatland Chrysler Library. The museum's collection includes one of the largest glass collections in the country, including works by Louis Comfort Tiffany. The Chrysler's collection of American and European paintings includes works by Mary Cassatt, Winslow Homer, Thomas Cole, William Merritt Chase, and John Henry Twachtman along with many of the French Impressionists.

Virginia Beach Visitors Information Bureau

2100 Parks Avenue
Virginia Beach, VA 23451
Tel: 1-800-VA-BEACH
www.vbfun.com

Norfolk Convention and Visitors Bureau

232 East Main St.
Norfolk, VA 23510
Tel: 1-800-368-3097; (757) 664-6620
www.norfolkcvb.com

WILLIAMSBURG

The Williamsburg Inn

Millionaire John D. Rockefeller's dream of creating a world-class inn in one of Virginia's loveliest settings became a reality in 1937 when the Williamsburg Inn opened for business.

Envisioning a "home away from home," Rockefeller became involved with every aspect of the inn's planning, from the lush landscaping to the Colonial [[au: not really Colonial, is it? not an era known for luxury; you say later it's Regency]] décor furnishings. The ambience of the white-columned beauty reflects the taste of the eighteenth century coupled with all of the amenities of the twenty-first.

An extensive multimillion-dollar renovation completed in fall 2001 recaptures the graciousness and style from Rockefeller's original plan. All of the inn's furniture by the Kittinger Company, a well-known maker of reproduction period furniture, has been re-upholstered and refinished. Guest rooms are designed in three styles: floral, classic, and restoration. Large marble showers, bath amenities by Floris of London, and Garnier Thiebault bed linens accentuate the comfortable luxuriousness of the inn.

The Williamsburg Inn: The front entrance to the Williamsburg Inn.
© *Colonial Williamsburg Foundation*

136 East Francis St.
Williamsburg, VA 23185
Tel: (757) 229-1000 x3089;
1-800-447-8679
www.colonialwilliams
burg.com
$$$$$
150 miles/3 hours

The inn reflects the style of early-eighteenth-century England with its deep moldings, antique furnishings, and silk window treatments.

The atmosphere of the Williamsburg Inn elegantly recaptures a Virginia country estate in the Old South. Nineteenth-century prints by John James Audubon adorn many of inn's walls.

Because of its proximity to Washington (150 miles south), the inn has attracted a host of distinguished guests throughout its history. Each room features a framed photograph of noted guests along with detailed background information.

Some names of note include England's Queen Elizabeth II and Prince Philip, Sir Winston Churchill, former President Dwight Eisenhower, and Emperor Hirohito of Japan. In 1983 one of the inn's most stellar events took place when President Ronald Reagan hosted the international summit of industrialized nations. The world event brought together Prime Minister Pierre Trudeau of Canada, Chancellor Helmut Kohl of Germany, France's François Mitterand, and Great Britain's Margaret Thatcher.

While the guest rooms offer the best in luxurious comfort, the dining rooms are every bit as appealing. The Regency Room borrowed period design elements from the Royal Pavilion at Brighton in England, including palm-leafed columns, crystal chandeliers, and leather-upholstered furniture. Hand-painted oriental panels and a tree of life design displaying peonies and birds are part of the decor.

Other treats in store include the Golden Horseshoe Golf Club—a trio of golf courses dotting the sweeping Virginia countryside—tennis, indoor/outdoor swimming pools, and the Tazewell Fitness Center.

Birders, bikers, and hikers can also enjoy the intricate web of trails, flanked by Virginia hardwoods, that surrounds the inn.

The Williamsburg Inn

ACCOMMODATIONS: Elegant historic inn with sixty-two guest rooms and suites. Tennis, golf, swimming, croquet, lawn bowling. Fine dining.

DIRECTIONS: Follow I-95 south heading out of Washington. Williamsburg is midway between Richmond and Norfolk on I-64 (take exit 238 off I-64). After exiting, look for green and white signs for the visitors center, which will direct you to the Williamsburg Inn.

Excursions & Diversions

While history ranks at the top of the list on a trip through Williamsburg and neighboring Yorktown and Jamestown, there are other sites nearby worth seeing.

The Mariners' Museum in Newport News, approximately twenty minutes from Williamsburg, and the Virginia Living Museum next door to the Mariners' Museum are both outstanding small museums.

The Mariners' Museum, one of the best nautical museums in the country, reveals a treasure trove of nautical artifacts. Vintage wooden ship models and figureheads as well as a detailed history of the Chesapeake Bay are just some of the many finds within its galleries.

The gleaming contemporary facility is a pleasant surprise on an outing and is recommended for anyone with an interest in the sea. Surrounded by nature trails in an unspoiled forested setting, the Mariners' Museum houses more than thirty-five thousand items including the anchor from the Civil War ironclad USS *Monitor*, Capt. John Smith's map of the Chesapeake Bay, and the polar bear figurehead from Admiral Richard Byrd's 1950s Antarctic expedition.

The collection of August Crabtree's miniature ship models is the museum's scene-stealer along with the prized marine paintings of John and James Bard, Fitz Hugh Lane, and Williams Trost Richards. Its galleries also offer an in-depth look at the U.S. Navy and the important role it has played in the nation's history. The accomplishments of Admiral Horatio Nelson, John Paul Jones, and David Farragut are also featured on a tour.

Within minutes' driving time from the Mariners' Museum is the Virginia Living Museum, where a winding boardwalk reveals the wildlife and plants native to Virginia.

The half-mile-long, elevated boardwalk crosses Deer Park Lake and weaves through dense woodlands. One can see fish in the natural stream, bullfrogs along the banks, and bald eagles, bobcats, deer, coyotes, and gray fox along the picturesque winding boardwalk trail.

Elaborate plans are under way at press time to expand the museum. A sixty-two-thousand-square-foot building with lots of glass will enable visitors to get panoramic views of the lush wooded setting. A two-level walk through habitat featuring a cypress swamp and an Appalachian mountain cove with an indoor waterfall are some of the highlights planned for the new facility.

A coastal-plain aviary showcasing the beauty of birds opened in July 2001. Pelicans, cormorants, egrets, herons, and ibis are some of the species found in the spectacular enclave.

Newport News Visitor Center

13560 Jefferson Ave.
Newport News, VA 23603
Tel: (757) 886-7777; 1-888-493-7386
www.newport-news.org

CHAPTER 6 *West Virginia*

WHITE SULPHUR SPRINGS
The Greenbrier

There are great hotels and then there is the Greenbrier. Standing like a proud mansion amidst a woodland forest, the resort quite simply is in a class by itself. The "grandest of the grand" aptly describes the Mid-Atlantic's, if not the East's, most opulent and grandest resort, which continues to cater to the carriage trade, diplomats, presidents, movie stars, and travelers desiring to experience history blended with style.

Tucked away in one of the most unspoiled and picturesque areas of the Allegheny Mountains, the Greenbrier carries the coveted Mobil Four-Star and AAA Five-Diamond honors. Owned and operated by the Richmond-based CSX Corp., the resort is just steps away from the meticulously restored Amtrak train depot (White Sulphur Springs is on Amtrak's splendid Cardinal route).

A National Historic Landmark, the Greenbrier represents over two hundred years of history with its striking antebellum architecture framed on a 6,500-acre resort. In fact, its lineage reads more like a novel than a short story, encompassing periods

An historic plaque with the stately AAA Five-Diamond Greenbrier in the background. *Trish Foxwell*

300 West Main St.
White Sulphur Springs, WV
24986
Tel: (304)-536-1110,
1-800-624-6070,
1-800-453-4858
www.greenbrier.com
$$$$$
243 miles/4 hours

from the Civil War to the Roaring Twenties, the Great Depression, World War II, and the Cold War.

The original hotel, which was built in 1780 and no longer exists, started the framework for White Sulphur Springs becoming a major tourist attraction. The warm mineral springs were the area's initial attraction. In 1858, the Grand Central Hotel was added to provide additional guest rooms. But the Greenbrier's true evolution into the world-class resort as we know it today can be traced back to 1910, when the C&O Railroad purchased and expanded the hotel. Construction soon began on the central portion, and by 1930 the Greenbrier, by doubling its size and adding amenities, was well on its way to becoming "the Palm Beach of Mid-Atlantic resorts."

The hotel's glamorous period of the 1920s and 1930s when millionaires, movie icons, and debutantes were the Greenbrier's economic mainstay came to an abrupt halt in 1940 when the resort was turned into the Ashford Army Hospital. The "grand lady of resorts" was reinstated as a resort in 1948 following a several-million-dollar facelift.

Its resplendent Gatsby-esque appearance is found in both its public and private areas. Its 638 guest rooms, 71 guest and estate houses, three championship golf courses, and an expansive spa have earned the Greenbrier the title "Resort of the Century" in Andrew Harper's *Hideaway Report.* And of course with all of this luxury comes the pricey room rates attached to a visit. However, its shimmering setting, excellent service, and flamboyant Dorothy Draper–designed interiors along with a wide range of diverse recreational activities make the resort more an experience than a place to stay.

From the moment guests step inside the colorful reception area designed in rich emerald green and hot pink, they are reminded that this hotel is going to be something extra special. An accommodating staff will go to great lengths in ensuring that a visit is pleasant, memorable, and, above all, perfect. One is quickly transported back in time to another era and instantly reminded of the famous people who have passed through the hotel's portals.

Few, if any, historic hotels can compare with the Greenbrier, which has catered to Civil War generals, the South's social elite, old money, royalty, and some of Hollywood's most famous names. Southern hospitality takes on new meaning at the Greenbrier, which sincerely makes all its guests feel as if they are royalty the minute they arrive. Doormen remember guests from years before, and waiters do not have to be reminded of a guest's dinner preferences.

Perhaps its most famous early guest was Confederate general Robert E. Lee, who traveled to White Sulphur Springs from his home in nearby Lexington, Virginia, in the summer of 1867. When the Civil War ended, a defeated and beleaguered Lee, who had assumed the post of Washington and Lee University president, made the trip to the posh mountain resort. For his first holiday since the Civil War, Lee came to the hotel at the insistence of his wife, Mary Custis,

President William Howard Taft vacationing at the hotel in 1908. *Greenbrier Hotel*

who was suffering from rheumatism. Like so many other guests before, the Lees believed the warm mineral springs to have healing powers.

Lee passed his first summer at the resort in the last cottage along Baltimore Row, which is today a small museum devoted to the hotel's illustrious history. His summer at the baronial resort consisted of parties, visiting with friends, and reading in the evening hours. Surrounded by his family and friends, the tired and aging general, in failing health, enjoyed perhaps the happiest summer of his life. His return to the resort for two summers following clearly paved the way for other famous guests.

It was at the turn of the century that the Greenbrier's reputation flourished, attracting the social elite. In 1908 William Howard Taft visited the hotel during his successful presidential bid, and in October 1914 Massachusetts millionaire Joseph P. Kennedy traveled here following his Boston wedding to Rose Fitzgerald. The Kennedys stayed for two weeks and Washington society soon followed.

But the Greenbrier's most celebrated and anticipated event occurred in 1919, when England's dashing bachelor, the Prince of Wales, later King Edward VIII, stayed at the resort on his inaugural trip to the United States. Much has been written about the charming English prince whose visit marked the beginning of several visits to the resort. He would return often to the West Virginia hideaway following his abdication from the throne in 1936 and subsequent marriage to American divorcée Wallis Warfield Simpson.

His initial three-day visit was to remain top secret and offer the prince a brief respite from constant press briefings and nonstop social events. Arriving incognito aboard a private railroad car, the twenty-five-year-old heir to the British throne witnessed a fluttering Union Jack flag upon his arrival at the hotel.

Occupying the entire third floor, the prince stayed in the same suite that President Wilson had occupied several years earlier. Every young lady within a hundred miles wanted to meet the bachelor prince. Being a natural and avid athlete, the young royal enjoyed the swimming pool, tennis courts, and golf course on his visit, where he also unsuccessfully tried to avoid the American press.

Returning during the 1940s when the hotel was a military hospital, the Duke and Duchess of Windsor visited with the soldiers who were patients. In 1948 the duke returned to the Greenbrier for its much heralded reopening following a major restoration and once again danced in the Cameo Ballroom that he had enjoyed as a youth.

Golfing legend Bobby Jones also traveled to the glamorous mountain retreat in 1924 and was one of the first golfers to play on the second eighteen-hole golf course. Other illustrious names associated with the resort include Sam Snead, Arnold Palmer, Dwight Eisenhower, Bob Hope, and Bing Crosby. The 1930s were another exciting period when Henry Luce, the Time-Life magazine publishing magnate, accompanied by his wife, Clare Boothe Luce, visited the hotel. Luce reportedly penned the play *The Women* during her three-day visit. Other guests of note include New York Yankees Babe Ruth and Lou Gehrig and movie legends Mary Pickford and Edward G. Robinson.

Presidents and millionaires aside, a new era began following World War II when, in 1946, a massive restoration project was put into place. Completed in 1948, the extensive restoration included sprucing up the hotel's fading interiors, repainting rooms, adding wings, and recruiting the designing talents of Dorothy Draper, who ushered in the familiar floral-themed interiors that remain today.

On April 15, 1948, fourteen private railroad cars brought such guests as Bing Crosby, the Duke and Duchess of Windsor, William Randolph Hearst Jr., and Mrs. Joseph P. Kennedy, with her daughters Patricia, Eunice, and Kathleen

The Duke and Duchess of Windsor dancing in the Cameo Ballroom at the Greenbrier 1948.
Greenbrier Hotel

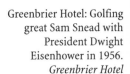

Greenbrier Hotel: Golfing great Sam Snead with President Dwight Eisenhower in 1956.
Greenbrier Hotel

and her son Congressman John Kennedy. They attended the much-heralded event that reinstated the Greenbrier's allure. The glittering Diamond Ball topped off the weekend's festivities. The hotel was back in business and wanted the world to know it. Once again the aging dowager became a glowing debutante, playing host to the Duke and Duchess of Windsor, who once again glided across the Cameo Ballroom.

The late 1950s and early 1960s were memorable years. In 1955 Debbie Reynolds and Eddie Fisher honeymooned at the resort, and in 1963 Prince Rainier and Princess Grace of Monaco and their children, Caroline and Albert, were guests at the Greenbrier. During the holiday at the hotel, Prince Ranier enjoyed rounds of golf while Princess Grace took long walks and carriage rides around the property. A portrait of Princess Grace now hangs in one of the sitting rooms off the main floor lobby.

During the Cold War the Greenbrier took on a new identity. Given the code name "Project Greek Island," the hotel became a top-secret government relocation facility during the Eisenhower administration from 1958 to 1961. The facility, built 720 feet under the West Virginia Wing, remained intact until 1992, when word got out that the Greenbrier had a bunker built within its confines. Daily tours of the bunker are now offered.

In January 1997 another former president, George H. W. Bush, toured the subterranean complex that had been so important during the Eisenhower administration. Following the September 11, 2001, attacks, many of President George W. Bush's key cabinet members, including Vice President Dick Cheney, were taken to the Greenbrier to map out strategy. Once again the grand hotel had made its mark in history, adding to its stature as an important and revered historical landmark.

Falconry, horseback riding, white-water rafting, mountain biking, fly-fishing, and golfing on three championship courses have ushered this "grande dame of resorts" into the twenty-first century. The shops and art colony on the premises offer one-of-a-kind gifts. Along the sweeping hotel corridors one can find the Carleton Varney shop, Polo Ralph Lauren, and the Greenbrier Shop, exhibiting everything associated with the West Virginia resort. The gingerbread Christmas Shop at the Amtrak depot, another unique aspect of the resort, displays every Christmas treasure imaginable for young and old alike.

Prince Rainier and Princess Grace of Monaco vacationing with their children, Prince Albert and Princess Caroline, at the hotel in 1963. *Greenbrier Hotel*

The Greenbrier

ACCOMMODATIONS: A grand resort with 639 rooms, 46 suites, 96 guest and estate houses, golf courses, pool, tennis, and spa. Rates include breakfast and dinner.

Directions : From the Washington Beltway take I-66 west to I-64 just inside the West Virginia eastern border. Exit 181 takes you to White Sulphur Springs and the hotel.

Excursions & Diversions

Approximately nine miles west of the Greenbrier is the Colonial town of Lewisburg, one of West Virginia's prettiest towns, sprinkled with antique shops and Colonial architecture. The scenic drive from the pampered world of the Greenbrier allows the traveler to see some of West Virginia's loveliest countryside.

Lewisburg, listed on the National Register of Historic Places, is an architectural gem filled with over sixty eighteenth- and nineteenth-century buildings that have been meticulously restored. The 236-acre historic district is lined with appealing shops featuring crafts, antiques, and rare books.

Considered West Virginia's premier cultural region, Lewisburg is filled with shops, inns, and charming country restaurants. The white-columned Carnegie Hall, one of only four Carnegie Halls still in continuous use in the world, is one of the state's leading cultural institutions and Lewisburg's architectural centerpiece. The 398-seat performing arts center showcases a wealth of talent from September through May. Classical music groups, dance troupes, and touring theater companies fill its busy calendar of events.

Robert's Antiques at 120 East Washington Street is one of the more upmarket antique emporiums, while Peddlers Alley offers collectibles of every sort. The Bookstore is for avid bibliophiles who are in the market for rare or out-of-print books.

For those inclined to outdoor activities, the Greenbrier River Trail is a must. Hiking, biking, horseback riding, and walking along the picturesque seventy-six-mile trail allow visitors to enjoy the Greenbrier Valley's geographic beauty. Consistently ranked by *Backpacker Magazine* as one of the ten top hiking trails in the United States, the trail meanders along the flowing

Greenbrier River, traversing thirty-five bridges and two tunnels. Cross-country skiers can also enjoy its winding pathways, which snake through the forested wilderness areas and end in Cass, a restored railroad town.

En route one can see a host of bed-and-breakfasts along with wild strawberries and blackberries, which grow plentifully along the wooded trail. Wildlife watching is also a good bet along this stretch of woodland where red fox, bald eagles, and beavers are often spotted.

Lewisburg Convention and Visitors Bureau

Tel: 1-800-833-2068
www.greenbrierwv.com

Greenbrier County Convention and Visitors Bureau

111 West Jefferson Street
Lewisburg, WV 24901
Tel: (304) 645-1000

CHAPTER 7 *North Carolina*

ASHEVILLE
The Grove Park Inn

A soft blue cast greets the morning light in Asheville. Located on the fringes of the Great Smoky Mountains, Asheville and the Grove Park Inn, its most historic hotel, reveal storied glimpses into both American and literary history.

The back porch area of Asheville's Grove Park Inn. *Trish Foxwell*

Largely associated with George Vanderbilt's palatial Biltmore Estate, Asheville is also the boyhood hometown of author Thomas Wolfe, who casts the longest shadow in the mountain town. Wolfe, whose look-homeward glances were never far from his thoughts, grew up in the town and captured his childhood memories in his first novel, *Look Homeward, Angel.*

290 Macon Ave.
Asheville, NC 28804
Tel: (828) 252-2711 or
1-800-438-5800
www.groveparkinn.com
$$$$
502 miles/8 hours

But many literary shadows are found here. Charles Frazier's *Cold Mountain* is a Civil War tale set in Asheville, and novelist F. Scott Fitzgerald traveled to Asheville in search of peace and renewal. Fitzgerald's Asheville days are closely associated with Grove Park Inn. An impressive cast of other American icons also retreated to the wooded mountain resort.

Hidden down a winding mountain roadway, the inn, constructed of large stone boulders, provided a welcome relief for the weary Fitzgerald, who had set up a temporary residence there while his wife, Zelda, received treatment at nearby Highlands Hospital. The gargantuan lobby seems likely to have attracted the Jay Gatsbys of Fitzgerald's generation, and indeed it did; Harvey Firestone and Henry Ford were regular guests of the inn in its heyday.

The inn's beginnings are as big and bold as the boulders that were used in its construction. The inn was built by Edwin Wiley Grove, a Tennessean and owner of a St. Louis pharmaceutical firm who became enchanted with the area on several visits. Grove hired a team of artisans and hundreds of Italian stonemasons and local laborers to realize his seemingly impossible dream of constructing a posh resort on the side of a mountain. The massive boulders that dominate the lobby's interior were taken from Asheville's Sunset Mountain and transported to the site by wagon trains.

On July 9, 1912, the official groundbreaking was held, and eleven months later, on July 12, 1913, the Grove Park opened its doors to the public. Not one to miss the chance for publicity and grandstanding, William Jennings Bryan delivered the keynote address, saying, "Today we stand in the wonderful hotel, not built for a few, but for the multitudes that will come and go. I congratulate these men. They have built for the ages."

The Grove Park Inn attracted important names from the beginning. Thomas Edison, Harvey Firestone, and Henry Ford, all friends and neighbors in Fort Myers, Florida, visited in 1918, arriving in caravans of touring cars. The Henry Ford group had traveled to the Grove Park Inn as part of a wilderness holiday that the men had mapped out, camping in Maryland and Virginia prior to arriving at the inn. Their visit was the final leg on their journey; they would head northeast following their visit.

Both Theodore and Franklin Roosevelt visited the inn, as did General Dwight D. Eisenhower, who spent hours on the golf course. Fred Seely, Grove's partner and son-in-law, met many of the inn's famous guests on his travels, including Herbert Hoover and auto magnate Henry Ford, whom he had met while working in Detroit in the 1890s. Seely also had made the acquaintance of Woodrow Wilson when Wilson was governor of New Jersey and had helped orchestrate his successful presidential campaign.

Other noted guests include financier John D. Rockefeller, who visited while overseeing the development of the Great Smoky Mountains National Park, golfer Bobby Jones, and best-selling author Margaret Mitchell (*Gone with the Wind*), who honeymooned at the inn in 1922 with her first husband, Red Upshaw. Enrico Caruso, Helen Keller, Harry Houdini, and Will Rogers, a friend of Seely's, stayed at the Grove Park while performing at the old Asheville Opera House.

But the most intriguing name attached to the Grove Park Inn is that of American author F. Scott Fitzgerald, who spent the summers of 1935 and '36 in rooms 441–443. Best known for his novels *This Side of Paradise, Tender Is the Night,* and *The Great Gatsby,* his most brilliant work, Fitzgerald traveled to the quiet village for a variety of reasons, not the least of which was that his wife, Zelda, was being treated at Highlands Hospital. He also came for his own health. It was believed that the crisp mountain air would prove beneficial to Fitzgerald, who was suffering from a mild case of tuberculosis.

Fitzgerald, a restless wanderer throughout his lifetime, envisioned Asheville as a peaceful haven where he could piece his fragmented life back together and reignite the creative brilliance of his youth. Refusing to believe his most creative and productive years were behind him, Fitzgerald hoped that in Asheville he could once again reinvent himself and recapture his flickering talent. His habitual drinking, high living, and constant financial woes had taken their toll and unfortunately followed him to Asheville. The Grove Park Inn did, however, offer the Jazz Age author a peaceful mountain respite and a second chance for better days ahead.

Fitzgerald remnants and reminders are found throughout the inn, most notably in rooms 441–443, where a small engraved brass plaque denoting Fitzgerald's residence can be found on the doorway. A combination parlor and bedroom, the rooms are ideally located near a stairway and the north elevator— both easy escape routes for Fitzgerald when he wanted to avoid the eyes of a curious public.

His days spent in Asheville centered around writing, sitting on the back veranda gazing out at Highlands Hospital, and engaging in lively conversation with the nearest beauty or anyone willing to listen. There is talk even today that the famous author had a series of dalliances with a host of women while staying here, but for the most part Fitzgerald kept to himself, often going into town to the library or trying his hand at writing in the rooms that became his sanctuary. An admirer of Wolfe, he donated a copy of *Look Homeward, Angel* to the local library.

The rooms where Fitzgerald lived reveal reproductions of the original Mission oak furniture that he used while living there. Although it is not known for certain if his desk was by the window overlooking the inn's driveway, it is certain that Fitzgerald spent countless hours writing and revising drafts in the room, with wastebaskets often filled with discarded yellow notes.

Fitzgerald's eventual departure from Asheville and the Grove Park Inn signaled an end to his marriage and ushered in a new chapter in both his personal and his professional life. His wanderlust took him back to New York and eventually to California, where he wrote his last novel, *The Last Tycoon*. In 1940, at age forty-four, the writer who had captivated a generation died of a heart attack in Hollywood.

The Grove Park Inn pays tribute to its most famous guest annually in September on or near the writer's birthday when "A Salute to F. Scott Fitzgerald" takes place. The week's activities include readings, literary seminars, and Gatsby-like parties.

While the inn has retained its historic lineage. it has added a few new and exciting additions. Since 1998 it has undergone a series of expansions and renovations under the watchful eye of Charles and Elaine Sammons, owners since 1955.

The spa, its newest addition to date, is constructed of high stone boulders in keeping with the architecture of the hotel; dual waterfalls and an elaborate skylight adorn its airy interior. A variety of treatments are available, and there is a daily use fee for both guests and nonresidents of the inn. The eighteen-hole golf course, designed by Donald Ross in 1924, has also been redesigned and spruced up, and the sports complex features six tennis courts (three indoor and three outdoor), a racquetball court, and an indoor swimming pool.

Its 510 rustic-design guest rooms, some offering panoramic views of the Blue Ridge Mountains, are found in both the main inn and the Vanderbilt and Sammon wings. A concierge-attended club level offers Continental breakfast and afternoon cocktails. A Mobil Four-Star, AAA Four-Diamond property, the Grove Park is close to Asheville's major sights.

In addition to the F. Scott Fitzgerald Weekend, the Grove Park Inn offers a variety of themed weekends throughout the year including the holiday season, when the gingerbread competition is one of the most popular. Fall weekend getaways, spa and golf packages, and wine-tasting weekends are additional opportunities to enjoy the mountain beauty.

The Grove Park Inn

ACCOMMODATIONS: A grand hotel and resort with 510 rooms including 12 suites, golf course, indoor and outdoor tennis, swimming, sports complex, and spa.

DIRECTIONS: Driving from I-40 south through North Carolina or I-26, take I-240 into Asheville. Take exit 5B (Charlotte Street), proceed north on Charlotte Street for approximately 1.3 miles, then turn right onto Macon Avenue; you will see the Grove Park Inn on your left.

Excursions & Diversions

Exploring Asheville is enjoyable any time of year, with the Biltmore Estate and the Thomas Wolfe Memorial the clear standouts on a visit.

George Vanderbilt's Biltmore Estate, North Carolina's most visited attraction, is a day's outing in itself. The 225-room French chateau mansion (not all rooms are open to the public) glorifies the Gilded Age with its ornate rooms filled with priceless antiques, furnishings, and paintings. The largest private home in the United States, Biltmore Estate is vast, so be sure to wear comfortable walking shoes while visiting.

A one-day pass admits one to the grand house, extensive gardens, and winery. The Biltmore Creamery on the site is the place to go for the best ice cream this side of the Blue Ridge. Expensive shops and a cleverly designed restaurant housed in a former stable ensure a memorable experience. A first-rate introductory film presented in the winery enables visitors to get a clearer perspective on and introduction to Vanderbilt's lofty vision.

The Thomas Wolfe Memorial in downtown Asheville is a must for literary enthusiasts. The Old Kentucky Home located at 48 Spruce Street was the childhood home of author Thomas Wolfe and the inspiration for his autobiographical novel, *Look Homeward, Angel*. A tour through the rambling Victorian home, named Dixieland in the novel, offers an insightful look into Wolfe's complex life. Rocking chairs accent the front porch, built in 1883; faded family photographs and original Wolfe family furniture adorn the house's interior. The most interesting room on a tour is the upstairs New York Room, which captures "Wolfe the writer."

Photographs of his editor, Maxwell Perkins, and his longtime love, Aline Bernstein, flank two typewriters, which he rarely used. Many of the items in the room were brought from Wolfe's apartment in New York's Chelsea Hotel. Books, kitchen utensils, a brown fedora, and a brass student lamp given to Wolfe by Bernstein accentuate the room's literary ambience.

A visitors' center, which shows a brief autobiographical film, and a bookshop specializing in Wolfe memorabilia can be found at the site. Other Wolfe-related sites in Asheville include Riverside Cemetery, where he is buried, and a life-size sculpture of a bronze angel given to Asheville by the Daughters of the American Revolution as a memorial to the writer.

Other Asheville attractions worth seeing include the Folk Art Center on the

Blue Ridge Parkway, which offers a treasure trove of mountain crafts, and the Asheville Community Theater with its Charlton Heston Auditorium. Another premier literary site can be found in nearby Hendersonville, where both the Flat Rock Playhouse and Connemara, Carl Sandburg's home, are located.

Asheville Convention and Visitors Bureau

P.O. Box 1010
Asheville, NC 28802
Tel: 1-888-247-9811; (828) 254-6102
www.exploreasheville.com

CHAPEL HILL

The Carolina Inn

The leafy college town, abundant with quirky cafés, art galleries, hoop dreams, and cherished college memories, is filled with many legends and stories.

The University of North Carolina, dating back to 1795 and the oldest state university in the nation, is Chapel Hill's architectural centerpiece. Colorful stories of Thomas Wolfe, its most lionized literary son, and Michael Jordan, basketball player extraordinaire and member of the class of 1986, are just a few of the famous names associated with Chapel Hill.

On most days a "Carolina blue" sky does indeed arch above the sleepy Chapel Hill campus, seeming to justify the old saying, "If God is not a Tarheel, then why is the sky Carolina blue?" The Tarheel State's most prestigious state university town is centered on Franklin Street, its busiest thoroughfare, usually filled with a flurry of cyclists and students, which cuts a swath through the middle of the parklike campus. Along the

The graceful Southern influences of the Carolina Inn's lobby area.
Robert Miller

211 Pittsboro St.
Chapel Hill, NC 27516
Tel: (919) 933-2001,
1-800-962-8519
www.carolinainn.com
$$$
525 miles/8½ hours

tree-lined boulevard guests will find the Carolina Inn, whose sporty appearance is a tradition in this neck of the woods.

Located across the street from the older part of the campus, the Inn is an ideal place for enjoying Chapel Hill's atmosphere. Affiliated with Hilton Hotels under the Doubletree banner and a AAA Four-Diamond and Mobil Four-Star hotel, the inn sums up Chapel Hill's history. Alums can be found lounging around the lobby area or in reading rooms that flank the main lobby.

The inn, owned by the university, is listed on the National Register of Historic Places. It is referred to as the "University's living room" by the locals, or, because it is so close to campus, the "plushest dorm this side of Franklin Street."

Opened in 1924 and built by University of North Carolina graduate John Sprunt Hill, the Carolina Inn was modeled after the Nassau Inn in Princeton. Hill believed that if the university that was so dear to his heart was to be in the same league as its northern counterparts, the town had to have a first-class hotel. The town sorely needed reputable lodging to house the visiting performers who were performing at Playmakers Theatre and noted speakers and dignitaries who were traveling through and to Chapel Hill.

During Hill's era Franklin Street was a mishmash of tired and dilapidated old boarding houses. Thanks to his tireless efforts and checkbook, the original Carolina Inn opened in 1924 with fifty-two guest rooms. In 1935 the generous benefactor donated the Carolina Inn to the university. In 1939 a major expansion took place that added forty-two guest rooms and a new cafeteria. In 1994 the inn underwent another $16.5 million makeover and expansion resulting in the relaxed and elegant setting visible today.

The Carolina Inn has played host to a list of luminaries including writer Eudora Welty, Margaret Truman, Jack Nicklaus, and Rose Kennedy. The inn's most interesting period occurred during the 1930s and 1940s. After the bombing of Pearl Harbor, with the nation at war, the inn became a major dining and lodging area for naval officers in training. The university's president Frank Porter Graham had close ties to the Roosevelt administration and offered up the university for the nation's defense to Roosevelt; with that offer came the Carolina Inn.

As a result, in 1942 the Chapel Hill campus, like many universities across the country, was transformed overnight into a barracks and training ground for the nation's military. Chapel Hill became one of four pre–flight training schools. More than twenty thousand servicemen lived and trained at the UNC campus between 1942 and 1945. Many of the servicemen preferred dining at the Carolina Inn, where food was much tastier than in the dorm cafeterias. This put an enormous strain on the inn and its staff but greatly impressed First Lady Eleanor Roosevelt, who during the war years visited the university and inn on several occasions to "look in on the boys serving the nation."

The first lady, who was forever indebted to both the inn and the university for their enormous contributions during World War II, gave a series of lectures, seminars, and conferences during her many visits, always choosing the Carolina

Inn for her accommodations. Never one to expect to be waited on, Roosevelt mingled freely among the soldiers and guests on her visits where she enjoyed the inn's genuine southern hospitality.

A star was born in 1953 when North Carolina native and UNC student Andy Griffith performed a show in the Carolina Inn's ballroom called " What It Was, Was Football." Griffith eventually became the beloved star of "The Andy Griffith Show."

The Carolina Inn's Crossroads Restaurant, a AAA Four-Diamond restaurant, offers a combination of Southern cuisine blended with American classics. The inn's Williamsburg décor emphasizes its southern roots, and its 184 rooms display a rich array of pastel-colored fabrics and chintz patterns. The Crossroads Bar and the Sun Room are also favorite spots for casual gatherings and get-togethers. Afternoon tea has also become a Carolina Inn tradition complete with scones and various blends of teas every day but Sunday.

Some other great dining spots in Chapel Hill include Mama Dip's Kitchen, a Chapel Hill landmark renowned for its old-fashioned southern fare: fried chicken, corn bread, and home-style vegetables. Sutton's Drugstore on Franklin Street, serving up juicy hamburgers and old-fashioned milkshakes, is another vintage Chapel Hill haunt and favorite of the locals; here the walls are decorated with mementos of UNC's glory days.

The Carolina Inn

ACCOMMODATIONS: Southern Colonal hotel with 184 rooms and suites on the campus of the University of North Carolina.

DIRECTIONS: From Washington take I-95 south, bypassing Richmond and heading to Petersburg. Take I-40 west from Raleigh to Chapel Hill exit 273B. Follow Raleigh Road/South Road through the campus. Turn right on Columbia Street and merge to the left lane, then turn left on Cameron Avenue, then left on Pittsboro Street; the Carolina Inn is on the left.

Excursions & Diversions

Exploring Chapel Hill and the surrounding areas is a cinch from the visitors' center off Franklin Street and to the right of Morehead Planetarium. Some recommended stops on your visit are the Ackland Art Museum, the More-head-Patterson Bell Tower, and the Old Well, the university's most familiar landmark. The Ackland Art Museum is of particular interest; a collection of paintings by Rubens, Delacroix, and Dégas can be enjoyed on a visit.

The North Carolina Botanical Garden on Old Mason Farm Road is the largest botanical garden in the Southeast and is ideal for hikers and nature-photography buffs. Consisting of six hundred acres of preserved land, it includes nature trails and herb gardens. The facility also features revolving exhibits of paintings and photography.

The Morehead Planetarium was the first planetarium in the South and is a teaching space for scientists, including the early astronauts. Show times and shows vary. Also on the Chapel Hill campus is the Morehead-Patterson Memorial Bell Tower. The tower was designed by McKim, Mead & White and given to the university in 1931 by John Motley Morehead. Its 10-bell carillon provides twilight music and serenades crowds leaving the Kenan Stadium following football games.

The Old Playmakers Theatre is a National Historic Landmark. The Greek Revival structure, built in 1851, is where writer Thomas Wolfe tried his hand at both acting and writing. During the Civil War when more than four thousand federal troops occupied the campus, the Union army used the facility as a stable for horses.

The Blue Heaven Basketball Museum is a must for basketball aficionados. Jerseys of the great Carolina basketball stars, trophies, artifacts, and Carolina basketball memorabilia can be viewed on a visit.

In Hillsborough, north of Chapel Hill and listed on the National Register of Historic Places, antique buffs can see more than a hundred late-eighteenth- and early-nineteenth-century buildings.

Chapel Hill/Orange County Visitors Bureau

501 West Franklin St.
Chapel Hill, NC 27516
Tel.: 1-888-968-2060; (919) 968-2060
www.chocvb.org

SOUTHERN PINES
Pinehurst

Whispers of the past linger like quiet shadows at Pinehurst. Dubbed the "St. Andrews of America," Pinehurst has been associated with golfing greats for decades. Ben Hogan, Sam Snead, Arnold Palmer, Tiger Woods, and countless others have strolled its hilly links in search of the perfect game. Bobby Jones and Walter Hagen also walked its hallowed greens, adding to Pinehurst's enduring mystique.

The front entrance to Pinehurst.
Steve Foxwell

Hidden in North Carolina's Sandhills region, one hour south of Raleigh, Pinehurst is quite simply a golfer's delight. Its undulating fields of green and memories of the great masters of the game add to its nostalgic atmosphere.

One Carolina Vista
Village of Pinehurst,
NC 28374
Tel: 1-800-ITS Golf;
(910) 235-8507
www.pinehurst.com
$$$$
347 miles/5 hours

New England millionaire James Tufts, namesake of Tufts University, who made his fortune in the soda fountain business in Boston, traveled to Pinehurst to escape the New England winters. In 1895 Tufts purchased five thousand acres of raw timberland and enlisted the architectural talents of Olmsted, Olmsted and Eliot (who also designed New York's Central Park) to carry out his plan.

The Holly Inn, a Queen Anne Revival cottage, was the first lodging facility built at Pinehurst. Heart of pine floors, a Scottish tavern, and a working fireplace enhanced its intimate and inviting appeal. At the inn's opening on New Year's Eve, 1895, $3 a day got one in the front door of the soon-to-be-burgeoning resort.

But it was Tufts's passion for golf and all that the game entailed that tugged at his heart the most. In 1898 he built the first nine-hole course at Pinehurst, and in no time the word spread that Pinehurst, with its year-round balmy climate and challenging golf course, was a first-class resort. In 1901 the Carolina Inn, often called the "White House of Golf," opened is doors, and in 1907 Donald Ross, who several years earlier had been recruited to be Pinehurst's pro, turned his talents toward developing course number two, and a golfing legend was born.

In less than twelve years what had begun as a scrub-pine flatwoods golf course became a popular winter retreat for wealthy families from New York and New England. Demand for additional rooms increased as Pinehurst's popularity grew, and in 1923 the Manor Inn was added to the list of Pinehurst's accommodations.

The Carolina Inn offers 217 rooms and 3 suites for visitors; the Holly Inn consists of 85 rooms. The Manor Inn, the smallest of the group, houses Mulligan's Sports Bar as well as 46 guest rooms. For lengthier stays, villas and condominiums are available for guests. The Carolina Inn, with its gleaming white facade set off by a copper roof, has been the favorite for discerning guests and professional golfers. Dominating Pinehurst's setting, the impressive building is complemented by the Holly and Manor Inns. All of the lodging choices exhibit a golfing theme. The Carolina Inn, the largest property on the premises, is the location of the Carolina Dining Room and the Ryder Cup Lounge, filled with Ryder Cup memorabilia.

Other dining choices include the 1895 Room in the Holly Inn, which vividly reflects Pinehurst's earlier era with its hardwood paneling, columns, and atrium ceiling. The Scottish Tavern is another favorite haunt for golfers with its authentic nineteenth-century Scottish pub and ornate English oak bar carved in Edinburgh, Scotland, in 1880 and displaying the original stained-glass and beveled-mirror inlays.

The Donald Ross Grill near the clubhouse where golfers tee off recalls the early 1900s. Here a time-travel photo gallery brings into focus the names of some of the golfing greats who have played Pinehurst. A spacious dining room with panoramic views of the magnificent greens adds to the experience. Outside the facility one can get a close-up view of the sculpture *Putter Boy,* Pinehurst's most beloved symbol.

Within a short walk from the Carolina Inn is the enchanting village of Pinehurst. Built by Tufts to give hotel guests a shopping venue, today the tiny avenue is lined with Victorian shops, including an old-fashioned ice-cream parlor.

Following Pinehurst's success at the turn of the century, some of the country's first millionaires, including Wall Street tycoon John D. Rockefeller, spent weeks at the North Carolina resort. Rockefeller is recorded to have spent several weeks in 1905, as did the du Ponts and J. P. Morgan, who loved to travel to all of the grand resorts on his holidays.

One celebrity not often associated with Pinehurst, cowgirl Annie Oakley, best known for her affiliation with the Buffalo Bill Wild West Show, was a regular guest at Pinehurst. Oakley originally came to Pinehurst with her husband, Frank Butler, to give shooting exhibitions and lessons at the golf club, but she grew so fond of the area that she and her husband spent the winters of 1915 through 1922 at the North Carolina resort.

Like Oakley, John Phillip Sousa enjoyed trapshooting on his visits. while Will Rogers, ever the horseman, preferred playing polo on Pinehurst's lawns. In 1931 aviatrix Amelia Earhart landed her plane on the Pinehurst airstrip prior to spending a holiday at the resort. Hollywood stars also made appearances at the resort. Silent screen star Mary Pickford, swashbuckler Douglas Fairbanks. and crooner Bing Crosby traveled to the secluded North Carolina hideaway for vacations. Crosby went anywhere there was a golf course, and Pinehurst, along with Pebble Beach in California, became one of his favorite courses.

Although there are many golfing stories associated with Pinehurst, the most famous one concerns Ben Hogan. Hogan, frustrated at not winning a major tournament in his seven years on the pro tour, finally got his big break at Pinehurst in 1940. He later went on to win the North and South Open in 1942 and 1946, breaking his string of bad luck. Hogan considered Pinehurst his good-luck charm and went on to win a host of tournaments following his wins at Pinehurst.

The names of presidents and diplomats are also listed among those of the resort's former guests. The Tufts Archives, a museum in the village detailing the history of both the resort and the village of Pinehurst, is a wonderful stop for seeing faded old photographs, archives, and assorted memorabilia.

Presidents Harding, Truman, and Ford, as well as army chief of staff General George C. Marshall, found their way to Pinehurst. Marshall purchased Liscombe Lodge in the village of Pinehurst in 1944. It is believed that Marshall mapped out the Marshall Plan while living at Pinehurst.

Near the clubhouse and Donald Ross Grill is a statue of Payne Stewart, who captured the championship on the number two golf course at the 1999 U.S. Open. Stewart is immortalized with a bronze life-size statue, the third statue to be added to Pinehurst's Walk of Fame. Statues of Richard Tufts, former president of Pinehurst and grandson of its founder, and Donald Ross, Pinehurst's first golf professional and noted golf-course architect, join him.

In March 2002 the Pinehurst Spa opened. Its newest facility, costing $12 million, the spa has elevated the resort's status to another level. With twenty-eight private treatment rooms and a state-of-the-art fitness center, the spa comes complete with a whirlpool, steam room, and sauna. Designed to match the Carolina Inn's original architecture, it is the largest spa built in North Carolina east of the Blue Ridge and promises to bring a new group of guests to the resort.

In addition to its great golf (eight eighteen-hole courses), Pinehurst, owned and managed by Club Resorts and the sister hotel of Virginia's Homestead, offers a host of amenities including bicycle rentals, carriage rides, and twenty-four tennis courts. Two outdoor swimming pools and Lake Pinehurst, a two-hundred-acre freshwater lake nearby, offers sailing, canoeing, paddle boating, kayaking, and fishing.

Pinehurst

ACCOMMODATIONS: Gold resort with 530 rooms including suites, villas, and condominiums. Spa, golf courses, outdoor swimming pool, tennis courts.

DIRECTIONS: Heading south on I-95 passing Richmond and Petersburg, get on I-40 from Raleigh; go east to U.S. 31 to Sanford and exit onto Highway 15–501 south to the traffic circle in Pinehurst. Once you reach the circle, take the second exit onto Highway 2 west. Follow Highway 2 for 1.3 miles and turn right; Pinehurst is straight ahead.

Excursions & Diversions

Believe it or not, there is more to Pinehurst than golf. The Weymouth Center, former home of North Carolina author James Boyd, is the area's main cultural center, offering activities such as literary seminars, poetry readings, art exhibitions, and concerts.

Another venue is the Pinehurst Harness Trace. Built around 1915, the course is open from October to May for spring harness racing, matinee races, and standard-bred training. Year round, early morning workouts are a great way for enthusiasts to see horses in action. Guided tours of the facility are available, and there is a trackside restaurant.

Just northwest of town toward the North Carolina Zoo is Seagrove Pottery, where visitors can see hand-tooled pottery crafted before their eyes. Salt-glazed stoneware displaying innovative designs is available for purchase along with an assortment of other creative items.

The North Carolina Zoological Park, ranked as one of the nation's finest, is another recommended stop. The wolf den and sea lion pool are some of its newer additions. Plan on spending an entire day here. There is a café, and a variety of interpretive programs are offered daily. A great spot for budding gardeners and botanists is the Sandhills Horticultural Gardens. Wetland trails and garden displays are the highlights here.

The National Register of Historic Places also recognizes the Malcolm Blue Farm, located in Aberdeen and built in 1825, as an excellent venue for a look at the rural history of Moore County. A farmhouse, old barns, a gristmill, and a water tower depict the area's past.

Southern Pines Convention and Visitors Bureau

P.O. Box 2270
Southern Pines, NC 28388
Tel: 1-800-346-5362
www.homeofgolf.com

Bibliography

Bailey, Diana. *The Mayflower: Washington's Second Best Address.* Washington, D.C.: Donning Co., 2001.

Berg, Scott A. *Lindbergh.* G. P. Putnam & Sons, 1998.

Conte, Robert. *History of the Greenbrier—America's Resort.* White Sulphur Springs: Pictorial Histories, 1998.

Johnson, Bruce E. Built for the Ages: A History of the Grove Park Inn. Asheville, N.C.: Taylor, 1991.

Page, Lee. *Pinehurst Stories: A Celebration of Great Golf and Good Times.* Southern Pines: Pinehurst Inc., 1991

Piedmont, Don. *Peanut Soup and Spoonbread: An Informal History of the Hotel Roanoke.* Roanoke: Virginia Tech Real Estate Foundation, 1994

Zogry, Kenneth Joel. *The University's Living Room: A History of the Carolina Inn.* Chapel Hill: Barefoot Press, 1999.

Index

A

Ackland Art Museum, 162
Adams, Henry, 72
Admiral Fell Inn, 51–52
African American History: Banneker-
Douglass Museum of African
American History, 44; Black
History Museum and Cultural
Center, 124
Annapolis, MD, 43–47
attractions: Banneker-Douglass
Museum of African American
History, 44; cruises, 46; U.S. Naval
Academy and Museum, 44
lodgings: Historic Inns of Annapolis,
45–46
restaurants: King of France Tavern,
45; Treaty of Paris Restaurant, 45
Antietam National Battlefield, 61–62
Antrim 1844 Inn, 66–67
Appalachian Trail, 127
Ashby Inn, 115–116
Ashe, Arthur, 118
Asheville, NC, 153–158
attractions: Biltmore Estate, 157; Con-
nemara, 158; Folk Art Center, 157;
Old Kentucky Home, 157; Thomas
Wolfe Memorial, 157
lodgings: Grove Park Inn, 153–156
Ash Lawn-Highland estate, 99
Astor, John Jacob, 19
Auchincloss, Louis, 99
Autry, Gene, 14, 34

B

Back Bay National Wildlife Refuge, 132
Baltimore, MD, 47–56
attractions: Fells Point, 51;
H. L. Mencken home, 55;
Harborplace, 51
lodgings: Admiral Fell Inn, 51–52;
Peabody Court Hotel, 53–54;
Radisson Plaza Lord Baltimore
Hotel, 48–50
restaurants: George's, 54; Lord
Baltimore Grill, 51–52; Owl Bar, 55
Banneker-Douglass Museum of African
American History, 44
Barley Sheaf Farm, 3–4
Barnum, P. T., 90
Barrymore, Ethel, 20, 72
Barrymore family, 90
Basie, Count, 28
Basinger, Kim, 87
Beatty, Warren, 120
Bedford, VA: attractions: National D-Day
Memorial, 128
Bellevue-Stratford Hotel. *see* Park Hyatt
Philadelphia at the Bellevue
Bennett, Tony, 28
Bergman, Ingrid, 34
Bernhardt, Sarah, 120
Best Western Independence Park Hotel,
22–23
Biltmore Estate, 157
Black History Museum and Cultural
Center, 124

Black Horse Inn, 113–114
Blue Heaven Basketball Museum, 162
Boar's Head Inn, 95–96
Bojangles, 120
Boldt, George Charles, 18
Booker T. Washington National
    Monument, 127
Booth, Edwin, 18
Bourse, 26
Boyd, James, 166
Bradley, Omar, 11
Brandywine River Museum, 37–38
Brandywine River Valley, 33–39
Brokaw, Tom, 72
Bryan, William Jennings, 126, 154
Buck, Pearl S., 8–9
Bucks County, PA, 3–9
    attractions: James Michener Art
        Museum, 8; Pearl S. Buck House, 7;
        Spring Craft Festival, 8
    lodgings: Barley Sheaf Farm, 3–4;
        Highland Farms Bed and
        Breakfast, 5–6
Bush, George, 146
Byrd, Charlie, 45

C
Calloway, Cab, 130
Carnegie Hall, 148
Carolina Inn, 159–161, 163–164
Caruso, Enrico, 154
Cavalier Hotel, 129–132
Chapel Hill, NC, 159–162
    attractions: Ackland Art Museum,
        162; Blue Heaven Basketball
        Museum, 162; Morehead-Patterson
        Memorial Bell Tower, 162;
        Morehead Planetarium, 162; North
        Carolina Botanical Garden, 162;
        Old Playmakers Theatre, 162;

University of North Carolina,
    159–162
lodgings: Carolina Inn, 159–161
restaurants: Crossroads Restaurant,
    161; Mama Dip's Kitchen, 161; 23
    Restaurant, 161
Chaplin, Charlie, 120
Charlottesville, VA, 95–100
    attractions: Ash Lawn-Highland
        estate, 99; Monticello, 98;
        Montpelier, 99; University of Vir-
        ginia, 99; wineries, 99–100
    lodging: Boar's Head Inn, 95–96;
        Keswick Hall, 97–98
    restaurants: Michie Tavern, 99; Old
        Mill Room, 96
Cheney, Dick, 84, 146
Chesapeake Bay Maritime Museum,
    65
Chrysler Museum of Art, 133
Churchill, Winston, 68, 81, 135
Civil War, 10–12, 118; Antietam National
    Battlefield, 61–62; Gettysburg
    National Military Park, 12
Civil War Center, 123
Clemens, Samuel, 18, 89
Cliburn, Van, 126
Clinton, Bill, 28, 84
Clinton, Hillary Rodham, 84
Connemara, 158
Coolidge, Calvin, 80, 89, 101, 130
Crawford, Joan, 87
Crosby, Bing, 58, 130, 144, 165
Cruise, Tom, 87

D
Dalai Lama, 96
Davidson, Arthur, 29
Davis, Bette, 130
De Haviland, Olivia, 80

Delaware Center for Contemporary Arts, 39
Dickens, Charles, 89
Dietrich, Marlene, 80
DiMaggio, Joe, 34
Dog Days at Oatlands, 117
Dorsey, Tommy, 28, 34, 130
Douglass, Frederick, 11
Doylestown, PA:
   attractions: James Michener Art Museum, 8; Pearl Buck House, 8
   lodgings: Highland Farms Bed and Breakfast, 5–6
Du Pont, Pierre, 33
Du Pont family, 165
Duvall, Robert, 108

E

Earhart, Amelia, 34, 72, 81, 165
Edgar Allan Poe Museum, 123
Edison, Thomas, 154
Edward, Prince (of England), 87
Edward VIII, 143. *see also* Windsor, Duke and Duchess
Eisenhower, David and Julie, 11
Eisenhower, Dwight D., 10, 14, 102, 130, 135, 144, 145, 154
Eisenhower Home, 12, 67
Elizabeth II, 87, 135
Ellington, Duke, 28

F

Fabergé, 124
Fairbanks, Douglas, 165
Faulkner, William, 99
Fells Point, 51–52
Festival in the Park, 127
Festivals: Dog Days at Oatlands, 117; Festival in the Park, 127; Spring Craft Festival, 8; Taste of the

Blue Ridge Blues and Jazz Festival, 127
Firestone, Harvey, 103, 153, 154
Fisher, Eddie, 146
Fitzgerald, Ella, 28, 45
Fitzgerald, F. Scott, 49, 53, 54, 120, 153
Folk Art Center, 157
Force, Juliana, 4
Ford, Gerald, 126, 165
Ford, Henry, 11, 103, 153, 154
Ford, Susan, 58
Fortner, Abe, 120
Franklin Institute Science Museum, 26

G

Gardens: Hillwood Museum and Gardens, 90; Lewis Gintner Botanical Garden, 124; Longwood Gardens, 37; North Carolina Botanical Garden, 162; Sandhills Horticultural Gardens, 167; Virginia Living Museum, 136
Garland, Judy, 130
Gehrig, Lou, 144
Gere, Richard, 87
Gettysburg, PA, 10–12
   attractions: Eisenhower Home, 12; Gettysburg National Military Park, 12
   lodgings: Gettysburg Hotel, 10–12
Gettysburg Address, 10
Gettysburg Hotel (Best Western), 10–11
Gettysburg National Military Park, 12, 68
Gibson, Charles Dana, 119
Gingrich, Newt, 84
Glenwood Park, 116
Goldwater, Barry, 11, 58
Golf: Ashville, NC, 153–156; Hot Springs, VA, 101–106; Southern Pines, 163–167; White Sulphur Springs, 141–149; Williamsburg, 135–137

Goodman, Benny, 28, 130
Goodstone Inn, 111–112
Gore, Al, 28
Governor Calvert (Inn), 45–46
Gowdy, Kurt, 58
Grable, Betty, 130
Grace, Princess (of Monaco), 19, 87, 146, 147
Grant, Ulysses S., 11, 89
Greenbriar, 141–148
Greenbrier River Trail, 148
Green Hills Farm, 8
Griffith, Andy, 161
Grisham, John, 96
Grove Park Inn, 153–156

H

H. L. Mencken home, 55
Haley, Alex, 44
Halsey, Bull (Admiral), 34
Hamlisch, Marvin, 28
Hammerstein, Oscar, 4, 34
Hammett, Dashiell, 49
Hardenbergh, Henry Janeway, 88
Harding, Warren G., 165
Hardy, VA.: attractions: Booker T. Washington National Monument, 127
Harley-Davidson Plant, 29
Harlow, Jean, 81, 130
Harriman, Pamela, 109
Harrison, William Henry, 11
Hart, Moss, 4, 5
Hawthorne, Nathaniel, 88, 90
Hay, John, 72
Hay–Adams, 72–73
Hearst, William Randolph Jr., 144
Henley Park Hotel, 74–75
Hershey, Milton, 13

Hershey, PA, 13–16
    attractions: Hershey Museum, 16; Hershey Park, 15; Hershey's Chocolate World, 15; Hershey Theatre, 15
    lodgings: Hotel Hershey, 13–15
    restaurants: Circular Dining Room, 14
Heston, Charlton, 96
Highland Farms Bed and Breakfast, 5–6
Hillsborough, NC, 162
Hillwood Museum and Gardens, 90
Hines, Earl "Fatha," 45
Hirohito, Emperor (of Japan), 135
Historic Inns of Annapolis (Governor Calvert, Maryland Inn, Robert Johnson House), 45–46
Hogan, Ben, 14, 163, 165
Holicong, PA, 3–4
Holly Inn, 163
Homestead, 101–106
Hoover, Herbert, 130, 154
Hoover, J. Edgar, 81
Hope, Bob, 14, 28, 144
Hopkins, Anthony, 97
Hotel du Pont, 33–35
Hotel Hershey, 13–15
Hotel Roanoke, 125–126
Hot Springs, VA, 101–106; lodgings: Homestead, 101–106; restaurants: Sam Snead's Tavern, 104
Houdini, Harry, 90, 154
Howe, Julie Ward, 89
Hoxie, Joseph, 22
Hull, Cordell, 86
Hunt Country Stable Tour, 116

I

Independence Hall, 25
Ink Spots, 45
Inn at Antietam, 60–61
Inn at Montchanin Village, 36–37
Inn at Perry Cabin, 63–64

J

Jackson, Mahalia, 126
Jackson, Stonewall, 113
James, Harry, 130
James Michener Art Museum, 8
Jefferson, Thomas, 98, 101
Jefferson Hotel, 76–78, 118–123
Jennings, Peter, 72
Joel, Billy, 77
Johnson, Joseph E., 113
Johnson, Van, 80
Jones, Bobby, 11, 144, 154
Jones, John Paul, 44
Jones, Robert Trent Sr., 102
Jordan, Michael, 161

K

Kalmar–Nyckel (ship), 39
Kaufman, George S., 3–4, 5
Keaton, Diane, 120
Keller, Helen, 154
Kelly, Gene, 80
Kennedy, Edward, 84
Kennedy, Jacqueline, 80, 107, 109
Kennedy, John F., 80, 107, 130
Kennedy, Joseph P., 143
Kennedy, Robert, 99
Kennedy, Rose, 14, 160
Kennedy family, 87, 144
Kerry, John, 84
Keswick Hall, 97–98
Key, Francis Scott, 11

King, Larry, 77
King, Martin Luther, Jr., 49
Kohl, Helmut, 135

L

Lamar, Hedy, 28
Langhorne, Irene, 119
Latham Hotel, 24–25
Lee, Robert E., 142
legionnaires' disease, 19
Lemmon, Jack, 120
L'Enfant, Pierre Charles, 71
Lenfest, Marguerite and Gerry, 9
Lewis, John, 86
Lewis, Sinclair, 72
Liberty Bell, 25
Lieberman, Joe, 84
Lincoln, Abraham, 10, 89
Lind, Jenny, 90
Lindbergh, Charles, 34, 72, 79, 120
Lombardo, Guy, 130
Longwood Gardens, 37
Luce, Henry and Clare Boothe, 144

M

Madison, James, 99
Malcolm Blue Farm, 167
Mancini, Henry, 28
Manor Inn, 164
Mansion Inn, 7
Mariners Museum, 136
Marshall, George, 11, 165
Marx Brothers, 4
Maryland Inn, 45–46
Mayflower Hotel, 79–81
Meade, George, 66
Mellon, Paul, 108
Mencken, H. L., 49, 55
Michener, James, 8, 57–58

Middleburg, VA, 107–117
   attractions: Dog Days at Oatlands,
      117; Glenwood Park, 116; Hunt
      Country Stable Tour, 116; Middle-
      burg Training Center, 116; National
      Sporting Library, 117; Virginia
      Gold Cup, 116
   lodgings: Goodstone Inn, 111–112;
      Red Fox Inn, 108–110
Middleburg Training Center, 116
Miller, Glenn, 130
Mitchell, Margaret, 154
Mitterand, François, 135
Monroe, James, 99
Montchanin, Alexandrine de, 36
Monticello, 98
Montpelier, 99
Morehead-Patterson Memorial Bell
      Tower, 162
Morehead Planetarium, 162
Morgan, J. P., 102, 103, 126, 165
Morris, Robert, 57
Morrison-Clark Inn, 82–83
Morse, Samuel, 90
Mosby, John, 107, 108, 115
murals of York, 28
Murphy, George, 80
Museum and White House of the
      Confederacy, 123
museums: Ackland Art Museum, 162;
      Banneker-Douglass Museum of
      African American History, 44;
      Black History Museum and
      Cultural Center, 124; Blue Heaven
      Basketball Museum, 162; Brandy-
      wine River Museum, 37–38;
      Chesapeake Bay Maritime
      Museum, 65; Chrysler Museum of
      Art, 133; Civil War Center, 123;
      Delaware Center for Contemporary
   Arts, 39; Edgar Allan Poe Museum,
      123; Franklin Institute Science
      Museum, 26; Hershey Museum, 16;
      Hillwood Museum and Gardens,
      90; James Michener Art Museum,
      8; Mariners Museum, 136;
      Museum and White House of the
      Confederacy, 123; Philadelphia
      Museum of Art, 26; Rodin
      Museum, 26; Science Museum of
      Western Virginia, 127; U.S. Naval
      Academy Museum, 44; Virginia
      Historical Society and Museum,
      124; Virginia Living Museum, 136;
      Virginia Museum of Fine Arts, 124;
      Virginia Museum of
      Transportation, 127; Woodrow
      Wilson House, 92
Myers, Hyman, 20

N
National D–Day Memorial, 128
National Historic Landmarks: Admiral
      Fell Inn, 51–52; Antrim 1844 Inn,
      66–67; Greenbriar, 141–148; Old
      Playmakers Theatre, 162; Park Hy-
      att Philadelphia at the Bellevue,
      17–21; U.S. Naval Academy, 44
National Register of Historic Places:
      Best Western Independence Park
      Hotel, 22; Carolina Inn, 159–161;
      Hillsborough, NC, 162;
      Homestead, 101–106; Hotel
      Roanoke, 125–126; Inn at
      Montchanin Village, 36–37;
      Lewisburg, WV, 148; Malcolm
      Blue Farm, 167; Mayflower Hotel,
      79–81; Morrison-Clark Inn,
      82–83; Park Hyatt Philadelphia at
      the Bellevue, 20; Pearl Buck

House, 8; Radisson Plaza Lord
Baltimore Hotel, 48–50; St. Regis,
86–87
National Sporting Library, 117
Nelson, Ozzie and Harriett, 28
New Hope, PA: lodgings: Mansion Inn, 8
Newman, Paul, 64
Newport News, VA, attractions: Mariners
Museum, 136; Virginia Living
Museum, 136
Nicklaus, Jack, 160
Nixon, Richard, 130
North, Oliver, 77
North Carolina Botanical Garden, 162
North Carolina Zoological Park, 167

O
Oakley, Annie, 165
Old Kentucky Home, 157
Old Playmakers Theatre, 162
O'Neill, Eugene, 34
O'Neill, Tip, 84
Oxford, MD, 57–59; lodgings: Robert
Morris Inn, 57–58; restaurants:
Robert Morris Inn Tavern, 58

P
Palmer, Arnold, 144, 163
Paris, VA: lodgings: Ashby Inn, 115–116;
restaurants: Ashby Inn, 115
Parker, Dorothy, 4
Park Hyatt Philadelphia at the Bellevue,
17–21
Peabody Court Hotel, 53–54
Pearl S. Buck House, 8
Peck, Gregory, 34
Perry, Commodore, 63
Pershing, John J., 86
Pfaltzgraff Pottery Factory, 29
Philadelphia, PA, 17–26

attractions: Bourse, 26; city pass, 25;
Franklin Institute Science
Museum, 26; Independence Hall,
25; Liberty Bell, 25; Philadelphia
Museum of Art, 26; Rodin
Museum, 26
lodgings: Best Western Independence
Park Hotel, 22–23; Latham Hotel,
24–25; Park Hyatt Philadelphia at
the Bellevue, 17–21
Philadelphia Museum of Art, 26
Philip, Prince, 135
Phoenix Park Hotel, 84–85
Pickett, George, 11
Pickford, Mary, 144, 165
Pinehurst (Holly Inn, Carolina Inn,
Manor Inn), 163–166
Pinehurst Harness Trace, 166
Poe, Edgar Allan, 52, 55–56, 99, 118, 123
Post, Marjorie Merriweather, 90
Power, Tyrone, 80
Presley, Elvis, 120, 121

R
Radisson Plaza Lord Baltimore Hotel,
48–50
Rainier, Prince (of Monaco), 146, 147
Rather, Dan, 72
Reagan, Ronald, 135
Redfield, Edward, 8
Red Fox Inn, 108–110
Remington, Frederick, 38
restaurants:
Annapolis, MD: King of France Tavern,
45; Treaty of Paris Restaurant, 45
Baltimore, MD: George's, 54; Lord
Baltimore Grill, 51–52; Owl Bar, 55
Chapel Hill, NC: Crossroads Restau-
rant, 161; Mama Dip's Kitchen,
161; 23 Restaurant, 161

restaurants (*continued*)
  Charlottesville, VA: Michie Tavern, 99; Old Mill Room, 96
  Hershey, PA, Circular Dining Room, 14
  Hot Springs, VA, Sam Snead's Tavern, 104
  Oxford, MD, Robert Morris Inn Tavern, 58
  Paris, VA, Ashby Inn, 115
  Richmond, VA, Lemaire, 122
  Roanoke, VA, Regency Dining Room, 126
  Southern Pines, NC: Carolina Dining Room, 164; Donald Ross Grill, 164; Scottish Tavern, 164
  St. Michaels, MD: Ashley Room, 64; Miles Room, 64
  Virginia Beach, VA, Orion's, 131
  Warrenton, VA: Inn at Little Washington, 114; Rail Stop, 113
  Washington, DC: Coeur de Lion, 74; Dubliner Pub, 85; Lafayette Room, 73; Victorian Dining Room, 82
  Wilmington, DE: Backstage Café, 39; Brandywine Room, 34; Green Room, 34; Krazy Kat's, 36
Reynolds, Debbie, 146
Richmond, VA, 118–124
  attractions: Black History Museum and Cultural Center, 124; Civil War Center, 123; Edgar Allan Poe Museum, 123; Lewis Gintner Botanical Garden, 124; Museum and White House of the Confederacy, 123; St. John's Church, 124; Virginia Historical Society and Museum, 124; Virginia Museum of Fine Arts, 124
  lodgings: Jefferson Hotel, 118–123
  restaurants: Lemaire, 122

Riggs, Bobby, 106
Riverwalk (Wilmington, DE), 39
Roanoke, VA, 125–128
  attractions: Booker T. Washington National Monument, 127; National D-Day Memorial, 128; Science Museum of Western Virginia, 127; Virginia Museum of Transportation, 127
  lodgings: Hotel Roanoke, 125–126
  restaurants: Regency Dining Room, 126
Robert Johnson House (Inn), 45–46
Robert Morris Inn, 57–58
Robinson, Bill "Bojangles," 120
Robinson, Edward G., 144
Rockerfeller, John D., 103, 126, 134, 154, 164
Rodin Museum, 26
Rogers, Will, 154
Rooney, Mickey, 80
Roosevelt, Eleanor, 27, 28, 102, 130, 160–161
Roosevelt, Franklin Delano, 14, 80, 102, 154
Roosevelt, Theodore, 154
Rubin, Robert, 77
Rubin, Ronald, 20
Russell, Rosalind, 34
Ruth, Babe, 144

S
Salinger, Pierre, 109
Sandburg, Carl, 11
Sandhills Horticultural Gardens, 167
Science Museum of Western Virginia, 127
Sharpsburg, MD, 60–62; attractions: Antietam National Battlefield, 61–62; lodgings: Inn at Antietam, 60–61

Shore, Dinah, 87
Sibour, Jules Henri de, 76
Sinatra, Frank, 14, 120, 130
Snead, Sam, 144, 145, 163
Soldiers, sailors, marines, and airmen's
    club, 82
Sondheim, Stephen, 5
Sousa, John Phillip, 165
Southern Pines, NC, 163–167
    attractions: Malcolm Blue Farm, 167;
        North Carolina Zoological Park,
        167; Pinehurst Harness Trace, 166;
        Sandhills Horticultural Gardens,
        167; Weymouth Center, 166
    lodgings: Pinehurst, 163–166
    restaurants: Carolina Dining Room,
        164; Donald Ross Grill, 164; Scot-
        tish Tavern, 164
Spacek, Sissy, 96
spas: Boar's Head Inn, 96; Grove Park
    Inn, 153–156; Hershey Hotel, 15
Spring, Dick, 84
St. John's Church, 124
St. Michaels, MD, 63–65
    lodgings: Inn at Perry Cabin, 63–64
    restaurants: Ashley Room, 64; Miles
        Room, 64
St. Regis, 86–87
Steinbeck, John, 4
Stewart, Payne, 165
Stoker, Bram, 19
Stuart, James Ewell Brown (Jeb), 108

T
Taft, William Howard, 101, 143
Taneytown, MD, 66–68; attractions: Get-
    tysburg National Military Park, 68;
    lodgings: Antrim 1844 Inn, 66–67
Taste of the Blue Ridge Blues and Jazz
    Festival, 127

Taylor, Elizabeth, 96, 109, 130
Thatcher, Margaret, 64, 135
Thomas, George, 20
Thomas Wolfe Memorial, 157
Tilden, Bill, 34, 106
Trudeau, Pierre, 135
Truman, Harry, 80, 101, 130, 165
Truman, Margaret, 160
Tufts, James, 163
Twain, Mark. *see* Clemens, Samuel

U
University of North Carolina,
    159–162
University of Virginia, 99
Upshaw, Red, 154
U.S. Naval Academy, 44

V
Vanderbilt, Cornelius, 103
Virginia Beach, VA, 129–133
    attractions: Back Bay National
        Wildlife Refuge, 132; Chrysler
        Museum of Art, 133
    lodgings: Cavalier Hotel, 129–132
    restaurants: Orion's, 131
Virginia Gold Cup, 116
Virginia Historical Society and Museum,
    124
Virginia Living Museum, 136
Virginia Museum of Fine Arts, 124
Virginia Museum of Transportation,
    127

W
Wanamaker, John, 19
Warrenton, VA, 113–114
    lodgings: Black Horse Inn, 113–114
    restaurants: Inn at Little Washington,
        114; Rail Stop, 113

Washington, DC, 71–92
  attractions: Hillwood Museum and
    Gardens, 90; Woodrow Wilson
    House, 92
  lodgings: Hay-Adams, 72–73; Henley
    Park Hotel, 74–75; Jefferson Hotel,
    76–78; Mayflower Hotel, 79–81;
    Morrison–Clark Inn, 82–83;
    Phoenix Park Hotel, 84–85; St.
    Regis, 86–87; Willard InterConti-
    nental Hotel, 88–90
  restaurants: Coeur de Lion, 74;
    Dubliner Pub, 85; Victorian Dining
    Room, 82
Washington, George, 115
Weaver, Sigourney, 96
Webster, Daniel, 11
Welk, Lawrence, 130
Welty, Eudora, 160
West, Mae, 90
Weymouth Center, 166
White, Stanford, 119
White Sulphur Springs, 141–149
  attractions: Carnegie Hall, 148;
    Greenbrier River Trail, 148;
    Lewisburg, WV, 148
  lodgings: Greenbrier, 141–148
Whitman, Walt, 90
Willard InterContinental Hotel, 88–90
Williamsburg, VA, 134–137
  attractions: Mariners Museum, 136;
    Virginia Living Museum, 136
  lodgings: Williamsburg Inn, 134–135
Williamsburg Inn, 134–135
Willis, Helen, 106

Wilmington, DE, 33–39
  attractions: Brandywine River Valley,
    33–39; Delaware Center for
    Contemporary Arts, 39; *Kalmar-
    Nyckel* (ship), 39; Longwood
    Gardens, 37; Riverwalk, 39;
    Winterthur, 37
  lodgings: Hotel du Pont, 33–35; Inn at
    Montchanin Village, 36–37
  restaurants: Backstage Café, 39;
    Brandywine Room, 34; Green
    Room, 34; Krazy Kat's, 36
Wilson, Woodrow, 89, 92, 99, 101, 143
Wilson, Woodrow (Mrs.), 11
Windsor, Duke and Duchess, 87, 103,
  144, 145
wineries, 99–100
Winterthur, 37
Wolfe, Thomas, 120, 153, 157
Woodrow Wilson House, 92
Woods, Tiger, 163
Woodward, Joanne, 64
Woolcott, Alexander, 4
Wyeth, Andrew, 38
Wyeth, Jamie, 38
Wyeth, N. C., 38

Y
York, PA, 27–29; attractions: Murals of
  York, 28; lodgings: Yorktowne
  Hotel, 27–28
Yorktowne Hotel, 27–28

Z
Ziegfeld, Flo, 90